Jay Ramsay is the author, co-a[...] of over thirty books of po[...] recently *Into the Further Reache.*[...] *British poetry celebrating the spiritual journey* (2007), *Out of Time.* *poems 1998–2008* (2008), *Anamnesis: the remembering of soul* (2008), *Soul of the Earth: the Awen anthology of eco-spiritual poetry* (2010), *Gita: a dialogue of love and freedom* (2012), and *Monuments* (2014). *The Poet in You* (2009) publishes part of his Chrysalis poetry correspondence course, which has been running since 1990.

Other poetry books by Jay Ramsay

Psychic Poetry: a manifesto
Raw Spiritual: selected poems 1980–1985
Trwyn Meditations
The White Poem (with Carole Bruce)
THE GREAT RETURN books 1–6:
The Opening / Knife in the Light: a stage-poem / The Hole /
In the Valley of Shadow: a cine-poem-cum-fantasy / Divinations /
Heart of Earth
transmissions
Strange Days
Journey to Eden (with Jenny Davis)
For Now (with Geoffrey Godbert)
Improvisations
Stories Beyond Words
Meditations on the Unknown God
Tao Te Ching (with Martin Palmer)
I Ching (with Martin Palmer)
Kuan Yin: the 100 quatrains (with Martin Palmer)
Tantrika: love songs of the Sixth Dalai Lama
Out of This World
Midnight Silver
like lightning inside lightning
Kingdom of the Edge: selected poems 1980–1998
Alchemy of the Invisible (with Genie Poretsky-Lee)
After Rumi
The Message (with Karen Eberhardt Shelton)
Chinese Leaves / Dream Whispers (with Genie Poretsky-Lee)
The Heart's Ragged Evangelist: love poems for the greater love
Local Universe: poems written in the Stroud Valleys
Out of Time: selected poems 1998–2007
Anamnesis: the remembering of soul
Gita: a dialogue of love and freedom
Monuments

Recordings by Jay Ramsay

Thread of Gold (with Rosemary Duxbury)
Night Road of the Sun: selected poems 1987–2003
Alchemy of the Invisible
Anamnesis (with Genie Poretsky-Lee)
Strange Sun (with Herewood Gabriel)

Places

of

Truth

Jay Ramsay

AWEN
Stroud

First published in 2009 by Awen Publications
Second edition 2012

This third edition published 2016 by Awen Publications,
12 Belle Vue Close, Stroud GL5 1ND, England
www.awenpublications.co.uk

ISBN 978-1-906900-40-3

For more information about Jay Ramsay visit:
www.jayramsay.co.uk

for Carole Bruce, Martin Palmer,
Donna Salisbury, and Aidan Andrew Dun

Contents

Foreword

Jay Ramsay is the most authentic poet I know. His heartfelt words connect fully with his deep inner self and with the reader or listener. He renews language with meaning, transforming it from the cheap coin of daily use, grubby and worn down, to something newly minted. The truth shines out. He is the heart's sincere ambassador and the mind's photographer. His poetry is punctuated by moments of gnosis that illuminate the secret processes of our inner worlds. He finds such moments in places, in people, in the negotiated territories between. At Britain's and Egypt's uncertain edges, Jay has charted the liminal in the quiet symphony of poetry.

In these poems Jay captures the distinctive genius loci of each place he visits. Such nodes of being are what he calls in 'Trwyn Meditations' 'places of truth' – places where 'you become real'. In 'By the Shores of Loch Awe', inspired by a stay in the wilds of Scotland, he suggests that 'the place is our language and our healing'. Here, as he and his fellow traveller head 'towards the farther shore', he finds 'the place of the heart's wild baptism'. Closer to home, 'The Oak' discovers a spiritual taproot in one of the oldest oaks in England, on the edge of the Cotswolds, which offers humanity some hard lessons. 'The Sacred Way' follows the Via Sacra of all pilgrims, the green road of the 'soul's way' across Albion. 'Culbone' is a mythopoeic excavation of a ninth-century church on the north Devon coast. Like most places of truth, it is small, discreet, off the beaten track, and resonant with numinosity – in Culbone's case, accreted over six millennia and imbibed by Jay over several visits.

Many of these places of truth only yield their treasures over time. One has to return to them with renewed perception to discover a new facet, another truth. The penultimate sequence in this book, 'The Mountain', ascends to the heights that offer perspective and clarity, the destination of rebirth, of love's release, the place of hard-won wisdom, a place that can ultimately be taken with you.

Finally, in 'Sinai', written during a stay in Sinai as a guest of the Makhad Trust in spring 2010, the poet goes into the wilderness like a desert mystic and experiences a deep communion with the song of Spirit contained within the silence: 'everything here held in God's peace'. Jay tracks his journey from the unreality of the entrepôt to the reality of the innerland, where 'There is another kind of life/beyond the road'. Arriving late, the weary traveller meets the threshold guardian: 'see ahead a solitary white figure/stand in the pale emerging moonlight/by a tethered camel … and we're finally out of time' and his Hero's Journey begins in earnest. Over the next few days Jay descends deeper into the silence and closer to the heart of the Mystery – which reaches its epiphany during a three-day vision quest. In a harsh but surprisingly feminised landscape ('Desert Vagina', 'Cathedral of the Breast') Jay encounters himself, his Self, and the Divine. The desert is the ultimate place of truth, where there is nowhere to hide. In the fertile void the pilgrim poet learns 'How to be with the time/what to do when there is nothing to do/and nowhere to go but here'.

The Sinai poems have a luminous lucidity that brings alive the desert experience in visceral detail, so that by the end we feel we have slept under the stars by a Bedouin fire and bathed in sand. We leave humbler, more respectful of our desert brothers and sisters, and closer to the heart of things. It is said you 'carry the desert with you'. And so it is with all places of truth: the wisdom gleaned lingers within you for the rest of your days. *Places of Truth* invites the reader to experience a different kind of travel – both inward and outward. Reading these poems makes me want to hit the road, to find my own soul places. They may bring out the Holy Fool in you also – and it takes an act of sacred craziness to be willing to step off the wheel of the world and choose the path of the pilgrim. Be warned: such journeys into the wilderness will challenge and change you. But by risking all we return immeasurably enriched.

To end with Jay's exhortation at Trwyn:

MAY YOUR SOUL
BE TOUCHED STRANGER
THE WAY OURS
WAS OPENED HERE

Kevan Manwaring

1

Trwyn Meditations

for Anthony and Gilly
at Plas Penrhyn
with thanks for Trwyn –
the wild, enchanted place below

Trwyn Penrhyn, a cottage isolated on the edge of Snowdonia and surrounded by forest, estuary, and sea, forms the setting of this sequence of poem-meditations written in a week in April 1986. They testify to the power of what is essential in all of us and what at the same time we are most in danger of losing. They include reference to the controversial 'cleaning up' of Y Gwyllt along with a poem written subsequently to help protest in the local area.

I was a regular visitor to Trwyn in the 1980s. The place was a revelation to me. No one I know who's been there has come away without being touched at a depth that is impossible to explain in a merely picturesque rational way. For me, the phrase 'place of truth' summons up best the image I have of its wildness and strangeness. You are what you are there. You become real.

1

Sunset
        the sky's light
                emptying into my eyes
– sitting
        blue touch my mind
                sky surround my
shoulders

sun enter
        between my eyes –
– water …
        a spring rivulet
                patterning the sand

the sea
        out of sight,
                a slight breeze

begins
        between my ears

– a curlew's cry
        the water's liquid note

down arms
        and legs
                to the earth's pull
                        rocking
gently
coming up under me –

– shouts
        across the Traeth
                roaring, clapping

that the silence
        absorbs

that the light
        like the water, pouring out

over the rock
        holds

that the being of this place
           draws back
                into itself

visibly hidden
        and in one
           sitting here

his body
        behind closed eyes
filled
        with the light's strength
                pumping through him

the body's vessel
        channel
          estuary-to-sea

body of light
        timeless as the sun

the blood's
        singing
           as his body, this place

ivy strewn

heart's
      breath

crown
      of sky

brow
      of these mountains

– tracing their line …

to wake and see

their each uplifted

breath containing

his sustained

deep spread

standing bow.

– A BILLION STARS
IN THE GREAT CURVE OF NIGHT
you could count them till you died

your head
tipped back
dizzy with their fire
their closeness
at the tips
of your brain's branches

their silver
leaves
their
silent pulse

their unknown
signals
circling life

.

. . .

.

the joined-
up dots
a child is drawing

and one of them
shooting across
slows to the naked eye –

far higher
than aeroplane or satellite
this star
that has no name

moving, steadily
across the Plough –

(light years ago
as the first rains fell
on this newborn
amoeba nebula
this unexploited
unfragmented
virgin
Earth)

3

– doing simple tasks:
breaking off
kindling
from a pile
of dead ivy

from
tree clutch
grip
unbreakable
creeping up
each tree's length

till the hands
that freed them came
and you
could feel
their relaxed
expanding

sixty foot
of tree being
bidding him welcome;
their sap
soothing his back,
leaning

to catch his breath –
quietened
among them to each
careful stroke
of the saw,
and then

the pulling snap
of each
tough-skinned vein
cleansing his
mind of its
weight of cramped

driven fear
freed, here
in this home coming
shared
between our eyes,
nod

no need to speak;
most things
have a habit
of sounding pompous
or trivial
in this place of truth

the essentials
are all we need
– it strikes me
how much
needs to be simplified,
how much
less said

when a nod or that
kiss of our eyes
from fifty yards away
is enough
or sitting
by the fire with
the dead ivy burning

and my body
slumped, stretched
back
at peace
with itself

– for once

is enough.

4

And then pain –
the head cloudy –
red behind the eyes
… burning

and it follows,
the way we are calmed
cleared, for each
unfinished business
of feeling to rise up
within us

– so watch yourself
observe
the lack of trust
the old enemy of time
forcing the moment
as the line breaks

in this forever
trying
to make words do
what they barely
in fact can –
and less and less
it seems
as the years pass
and their
fragile autonomy shrinks
as the mystery
around them
closens and increases;
and the world
they are here for
becomes more real

so they become what they are:
hammer and liquid chisel
the breath's clothing
that each gesture
of the body
is constantly outliving –

so when you speak
I look for you always
at the end of what you say
through a glass darkly
and then face to face.

5

I am,
and yet to learn
to be what I am *not*
where I have no faith
is where my whole faith founders,
where I threaten it
with unconsciousness
where I seem to be most
conscious: of my rage today
at the rape of this forest
napalmed for timber money
tamed to some smugly safe
sentimental Nature trail
and as we stand, and I hold
this lump of charred wood
in my hand – who should walk by
but three assenting materialists
admiring the tidiness
of the devastation
you say projection
& I say I wish I had
projected this lump of wood
onto one of their heads
and if you stood me in a mirror
I would say the same again
until it hurts
as it does now,
the raw lopped trunks
the shocked surviving trees
as powerless as I am
enraged, or detached?
Do I chainsaw myself
with this anger? Do I
only add to the place's blood?

I do not know enough
about withholding;
I have little faith
in letting these things go
in letting the wrong
unravel itself
around the wrong doer
in letting time
effect its justice
on the killers
I am called upon
to heal and bury

6

for Carole

Love, oh love, oh fearless love –
the place is now, its wasted memories
blown away like fine sand –
the clean picked shells, the keen wind's

wavering upstream lifting your hair back,
swinging upriver to the snowswept peaks
and round – gliding down – your eyes scanning
our unhurried steps from the light's high breath

you loosed your being into –
letting your body drift, your heart open
like a spinnaker, and everywhere your eyes looked
– there you were, rock and sea and sand skin

blending and unfolding –
from the birth you were given, to each birth
you have given, every day to every care-filled
compassionate atom

to come through your darkness and have
the whole unforeseen sudden joy of it given back.

7

Low tide ending, and now the twilight's silver sunlight,
standing at the clifftop; windless, calm as a black-
headed gull circles its gliding shadow across the curving
inlets of mud among the straw coloured reeds

across where the water mirrors the living sky's inner
stillness in reverse …

mirroring what we are continually in each day's changing
cloud and eye and mindscape, heartscape of rain and
green and grey and sun:

gathered and packed, shouldered in this sealed quiet,
silence full of speech deepened in its unbroken flame-
like candle steadying

and all around – villages, town and mountains – then
web of light we are connected to, the life we are
returning to,

and still there is no leaving and no ending

place of truth
outpost
the Earth
without us
would as gladly
return to

as the shadow of the bird for a second becomes a
fighter plane ripping across the New Year sunset –

as somewhere
the flung bottle

washes ashore with this writing

MAY YOUR SOUL
BE TOUCHED STRANGER
THE WAY OURS
WAS OPENED HERE

– as we turn

together

to go in peace.

Trwyn Penrhyn, Porthmadog, North Wales

2

By the Shores of
Loch Awe

for the place —
its uncompromising oneness,
wetness, and greenness

and for Carole,
my companion there

More things are learnt in the woods than from books; trees and rocks will teach you things not to be heard elsewhere. You will see for yourselves that honey may be gathered from stones and oil from the hardest rock.

St Bernard of Clairvaux

1

The ribbon of road,
Unwound like spilt tape
Stretching back –
And what we were driving towards …

As you gestured over to the place of your birth,
Invisible in the hot misty distance –
And then, as the engine spluttered, slowing,
Rattling … as it steamed – and cracked,
Rod-spun, bits clattering on to the tarmac

Moments, a mile later. And is it ever
What you thought was happening?
The journey is its own; and we journey it.
Even before we do? Or it thickens around us
Weighing the balance, and waiting

For the next word, phrase, thing. Green doors.
A pit-tanned droll smiling face, and a white van.
A white van for the borderlands, and we're in it.

This is the land. This is the country …

The rolling, curved, veined sheep-dotted hill heights,
Heavy blue haulage – visible alchemy
With its tank-wheels, and escort
(coagulate, grinding uphill under the sky)

As the land builds. To the Increase. Remember.
To the Lakes … and can you think like water?
Fluid, swirling – soul – become as it
Dissolving into grey by twilight water

Leaden-limbed, drawn down into it; lapping
All the sheep-loud night before dawn …

And can all we are of heaven and earth
Combine now? Told, this is the time, now
'And as I make love to you, I give you heaven
And as you receive my love, you give me heaven'

Or, you say it: 'the strangeness of truth'.
The strangeness of a tree within a tree.

Northwards, towards the border –
And the truth is a rear-view mirror
(patched on, drooping, in red tape)
And the law is: everything signifies

And can you read the signs?

To see back, without being swamped –
And can we hold this moment
Without the past breaking in?
Can we risk ourselves

Without hiding, or pretending?

As it flows towards us. Its edge. Ever-closening
(outside us now, here now, at its mercy)

Its gateway: twin windowless turrets
Of pale red stone – flanking the road:
Pulled into her heart, and lifting him out

As the land opens. Flat. Wide open. Zone.
Yellow gorse flowers, and sunned dry grass;
Pylons, and distant pines
                                    strangely light

And still, it could be anything
Still-lit ... blanked words ... *Boreland*

But it means, ahead is a great country
And we are for the Great Water's crossing

We are for the earth – these mountains
Slowly rising
                              as if dreamt

Rugged, forested, green summits
These mountains of the heart, by their names
Ben Arthur

The forest in your heart I wanted to embrace,
Cracked open, a little wider … and on the ground
Shirt-blown, lying

Where we were two saplings, barely rooted,
Like straw in the blast; and it held us
And was father
                              was a father, too

– I never knew the heart could be so big
   So limitlessly mountainous, and without pride
   Holding the smallest yellow flowers
   And with the sky at one, above it –

Lingering, spelt in your hand … as it suffused in,
Quietly, overwhelming us beyond us
With the strength of its gentleness
                                        green, grey

Sky darkening before rain, slate by the loch
(where the gulls were white, vivid, flung, flying
against the sky they merged to)

In this far country of the eagle

Where Castle Stalker stands
Alone on its island
With its single slate-wet turret

And the bird, with its great shaggy wings,
Spreads against the pearl-blue heaven of cloud

Above the ribbon of road
                              and the first drops of rain.

2

The brown sail of the tent
Unfurled, spread — stretched and pegged
Behind a thin wind-screen of trees –
And a briny, effluent stream. Loch edge.
(As close as we could get.)

Before the rain set in. And the dark.

The water gleaming through the green-leaved beeches ...

And the dark like no dark you could see,
Only darker. *Night.* And the race
Over the hissing black headlit road
For fourteen miles, for food – for nothing.

For being here.
(Heating up soup in a swarm of midges
 In the back of the van)
Is being stopped.

To earth. Survival earth. And after rain, mud.
And the water carrier burst –
Sampling the tea-coloured stream,
And squatting on our heels,
Like the first here.

Like Beaker People. Like Indians.

(And over to our right, Crow Island.)

And the loch in the sun like the sea ...
briefly

My mind of fire is dying;
Someone put it in among some stones
Before we came, in a charred tight circle
In among the blackened remains of kindling –

When your fire has purged and bared you,
It has done its work. Let it go, now.

It is not what is needed here.
But a mind of earth … in the beginning.

And yours is water and feeling,
Say our invisible parents: and it's fragile,
To be slow, or as quick, to miss the point –

To force it into 'being good'
To deny each other what we deny in ourselves

To be like strangers, and to ourselves –
Given this chance, this place

To feel what wrongs the sunlight
                                        as it slips

And how easily the whole foundation shifts,
As if kicked –

And bow to it: clouded over: broken
As we gather the white quartz stones
To make a circle, with a heart-stone –
A hearth stone – at its centre

On a bared scrap of grass, where a fire was
(Vanished now): stone by stone, laid, placed

'And that the white
　　　　that the light
　　　　　　　　brought to earth
Become rock that holds,
　　　　rock that heals'

　　　　*

– you walking … green, like an answer
green everywhere
　　　　　green in the light

Bracken – ferns – bog iris stalks

now we walk this road
　　　　with the loch beside us

green bathing our eyes – among spots of colour,
rosebay willowherb, pink sorrel, and foxgloves;
hushed to a black butterfly, poised –

with its dark red fringe-of-wings
spread, quivering; and white
dotted encircled glyphs
　　　　on either wing

a perfect square of lichen-covered rock

and in the rock, where it rises, sheer –
in a cleft in the rock, narrower than a finger
a sprig of beech
　　　　fresh, with its leaves

a beech tree in miniature
　　　　under the sky

dove-greying, like the water

*

As the light slants,

        shifts,

                slides towards rain

And our demons come and go;
Wrestling them: to name them:
Mistrust, Fear, Control

And to realize how our words
Use us, thinking we use them
And how to speak heart

Attuned to its silence, its space
That silences you –
To find yourself surprised,

To find yourself as if belittled,
Small as you are, new, becoming
Now – as its moment is – (and can
You turn yourself around?) as fast
As that old unwanted self reacts back

                to that edge
Thread, of its again-finding, or loss –
And how you said it when you said,
'When I go into my head, I lose God,' every time –

And to find Him here
In the sound of the stream, the wind in the leaves,
That owl, hooting …

And you found Him
Like you lose Him,
Like you lose your heart –

'So may we be open here'

                (and I found you, in the dark).

3

Wet chrysalis. Wet womb chrysalis,
Waking to it, and to this –
Raw closeness, and of earth. Death, is it?

Or greyness, leading to green;
Grey water, the loch glassy –
The loch, a mirror.

Grey voice, thread silver: whisper
The loch's inflowing, and the leaves,
Behind these eyes, become a throat
Stirring to speech.

And green is death, too,
Into the blackness, and out of it:
Yew shadow, evergreen

                mystery of green

Of grey, edging, invisibly –
Essence of invisibility

                merging visibly

– the sheep, standing, staring
grazing among the trees

                nosing closer
black-nosed, innocently

                nibbling at the branches

with the water behind them …
behind their eyes

                staring into mine

with what never dies –

This place, alive with all its memory

                      invisibly

Ancient as its first comers,
Its clawing glaciers –
Its sacred overflowing spring

                cascading

crystal, down

Ben Cruachan, now
Its power station hidden,
Its rising twin peaks
Creviced by a waterfall

High under its static smoke-fleece of cloud,
High green, and the line of its waterfall
Cloud-light, white trailing, moving as in a dream

And under the mountain
(as the road bends road)
On its faery islet – Kilchurn, in the sun

Belying its own history,
Its Campbell shell
Imaged in false light

Beside St Conan's, built late,
Inside its corbel of owl-like sphinx-like
Gargoyles – is light, feminine light
(where the Bruce lies dreaming in waxwork stone)

The pulpit, with its encircled cross,
And where the altar would have been:
A plain empty table: plain, unstained windows
With the trees for green they reflect

Green tree-light, Cathar light,
A church for women, and the pew you sit in
For the healing of time ...

Carved towards the loch, on its parapet edge
Of raised stone, one stone for each word
Thy / Sun / Shall / Not / Go / Down

He said

– even in the rain
     in the grey of Oban

Columba's green, beckoning
       and the green etheric

spread over the land
     like a single tartan

and what stands out in it, alive –
soft brown Highland cattle
and a pair of swans on Loch Etive
(distant, specked ... towards the farther shore, together)

and the cloudscape and mountainscape,
       blended
and the tip of mountain and cloud
    drawn down towards each other –

Places so small they could be a hoax

And at Cladich, the river there
Under the bridge: tanned coloured peat water
Rushing, pouring: the surface slipping down,
Rock-strewn, to a scur of white foam

— white foam, out of tan water

        two thick tongues of it

the river, tawny

    the river, a wet lion —

Divining the future in swords
And the way through a lightning-struck tower
The way the tunnel is yours, now,
And the tower

Bared to its bone, its foundation:
We become like a falling landscape
Of inner monoliths, crumbling
In this exile of ourselves, alone, for real

Withering to the truth, and the taste of whisky
Malt-soft, like fire —
(instead of the wood, too wet to burn)

And the rain, the rain unceasing
All night in the tent-spattered dark

And the burn, with its drumming gurgle
Where the water comes down over stones

And in the dark, voices,
Voices, but you could not hear them,
Voices, in the water — or in the air around

Shouting, singing, high-pitched as the Sidhe
As if before a catastrophe —
Ghosting the downpour

       you shivered awake in

(in the darkness of wet
                    you drew me to
come, calling out
                to the stream
where its water
                reaches the loch's incoming

long, wide, wavelets …)

… gouged to the root
Of our blackened-out bodies
                    splayed like a
                            black womb-flower.

4

The song, sung to the bone.
And the song is feeling and flowing.

Stillness. Breathing. Seeding

(And how are we, moment to moment
                                        changing
  So the place is
                as we become it)

To see how the placing
Of every stone and branch
Makes the stream's song

Stone by stone, as they
Angle and dip, brown-stained
And the stub of a beech

A sapling sprouts from
That the water swathes around
To where it splays into the loch

(And the tent's skin, in the breeze
 Imprinted with tree-shadows ...

And in the van's side mirror
 Branches, and a patch of blue sky cloud
 As strong, or stronger, than my own face)

By grace. By transparency.
By a light stronger and gentler than anything.
And if you walk that way, you will be kind.

The sun, shining on the grass ...

– and the dead skins of the kippers
turning in the wave
                    floating in the wave

are bronze treasures
                    in gold light –
The loch inside us, like them.
And gone beyond words, we wonder.
If this is the beginning or the ending
                    or neither

– turning in the wave,
                    turning in the deep

of the unseen peat-black water …

– The passing fields,
Their wound still-green mats of hay

The knife of rain-silver light
Thrilling the clouds and the mountain-rim
Slowing along beside it

Slowing to stone at Kilmartin –
Thirteenth, fourteenth century gravestones
With their swords and tracery, armoured

Knights, faceless in vizored grey
Ghost-grey – each facing both ways –
Armed at the front, with chain-mail and spears

And facing behind them, into the unknown:

Warrior, what will come out of the mist to you?
Will your claymore and spear be of any use?
Is it a spear you need now, or a staff?
A vizor, or a cowl?

(Your soul, grey, armourless, waiting)

And the great cross inside the kirk
With Christ, skinny, skeletal, crucified,
His arm fragmenting into metal stanchions –
Crowned above with a distant angel

And on the other side of grey, grey
He is Risen, risen through the centuries –
Now comes the resurrection ... the missing piece
Unearthed, under a raised pick –

Become annunciation, where the fracture
Cuts across His face and open eyes
Shining, worn, almost invisible in the flash-light:

Master, born out of the ground,
Mother, Madonna, and the earth like a sun,
Earth, risen – earth, a sun –
In her belly and in her rising

                                    come

Master of death, mother of death, come

– risen, like the necklace

                        bead by bead

out of the cist,

                    under the elm tree

threaded, hole by hole, with tiny rootlets –

(around your neck and your warm bare breasts)

And the dead in their sleep of stone,
Under a lip of stone, at Dunchraigaig –
Bent, to their sideways gaze –
Charred bones, gone into the labyrinth

Deeper and deeper into matter
Down the years, down the centuries

Down this Via Dolorosa of tears

– to the depths of stone
                              in our eyes
blue clay
            blue clay sea-dreaming depth

in the mystery of bone and sea-flesh
that the farmer forgets, that the field forgets
cordoning their standing ...

and we remember
                  stilled to this stone, blood-dark

breathing the breath of its grey breath

(two sparrowhawks hovering)

Awake in the Land of Pain,
The gouged furrows in the hillside
As if combed with steel –
(For peat, or planting)

The earth dry, bared in the green
Lashmarks on the land's flogged back
And in us, as the road wound
Through the wound of it, acre after acre

And we sit here, we sit naked here,
There is no escape, only the silence
And the pain, before the pain can shine
The soul's way, out –

Love, in your eyes

(And the sun-stone they sharpened their blades on
 Stands like a man in prayer)

– before the green echoes back
                                    open, towards the sea
bracken, couch grass
                        blending, unbroken
light-shaded
                with outcrops of heather-mauve

like something already healed –

Coming down, through the forest
Past an upturned stump with its roots bared
To the sky: pines, pines, pines …

Pausing to find where we are,
On the other shore – standing
On a forestry bench, to look down

Bird-wise at our size,
The way the sky might look at us
More closely than we imagine …

Among the miles of forest and inlets;
Down to Ford … and back to drying blankets,
The tent glowing with two lit candles

The rain whispering down among the leaves,
The loch in the grey-silver light, as it always was,
And the flitting, curving, diving

– black blur of a bat
                        hurtling fast aside
and circling –

And the water, patient to its reflection
Spelling: wait

And deeper than anything we can say now

    the place is our language and our healing.

5

To let it be now,
Given as it is —
Sinking like the rain
Slowly to its depth.

When there is space between us —
We can be essential, giving
And given to, like the rain to the ground,
And the sun to the grass, to the sheep.

We are figures in a landscape, if we know our place.
And the letting be can breathe as it can smile,
Thanks to a passing driver —
Waving, to a fellow walker.

We are the key and the core
And there is more in woods and stones
Than in books —
This is the book I am reading.

The loch, its spine.
The ground, its pages.

And for you, it's all colour
You confessed to despising —
Black and white, all form and tone
Transformed, come through, come alive
To what matters: not the photograph

Become its own transparency —
The elements, its developer;
The night, its darkroom: the print
Of it, unique to each pair
                                    of seeing eyes

– to find words for *that*.

'To see your birth in everything'
(And you handed him an egg).

To be a priest of earth.
Across the narrow causeway
Of half-sunken stones –
Where the temple stands, bruised by fire;
The trees, abused – their hollows, burnt –

To dare to be your heart. And be it.
To make this cross out of branches and stones.
To speak the words. To be oak.

Heal us.

And what binds us is what frees us –
The knot of the cross,
                                        the heart bound to earth
Bound?
            to love.

Free, as the loch
Free of the blood that bled
Free of the hunters –
Free of the jolly paddle-steamers

Freed from time, in time, through time

The castle where they imprisoned the child
The Castle of the Red-Haired Girl
The ford where the warring brothers both died
(The pass with its staked line of heads)

The banner, snaking up into the air!

– falling
                    plunging down among the trees
up the
          slippery mud-path, holding the wire –

(the roar, returning
                    pure, cleansing
                              like thunder)

The herd, lowing, noses raised, along the road

Fincharn, fired, and buried in ivy
(like a folly, across the bull-field now)

And if you come here, in the rain
As we came off the map by the edge of the road
To a wet tractor-track leading up out of sight,
Slow walking, steep, rutted among stones –
The old path, long unused, untrodden

If you come this way, in the pine-scented air,
In the quietening, gathering, waiting air,
You may feel something coming to meet you
Stirring under your feet and clearing in your eyes
Though there is nothing you can see

But pines and bracken; until you glimpse – walls,
Fringing the green – low, bleached, lichen covered
Walls, and a skirting wall where the gate once was:
And we paused there, without knowing why –

Wading through the bracken, to it –
To the left portal with its Devil's Handprint

To gaze at it, roofless, among fallen masonry –

Overgrown, now given back:
                    given to bracken, to ragwort
Flowering, thistle-heads, bees – and a butterfly
Given in the arms of a dead tree, leaning
By the far wall, with one branch of it alive –

Given to light, and intact – the font intact,
Aumbries and piscina, and our steps
Unsure of what we were about to tread on;

Stone, or earth, or gravestones – carved, abandoned
Asleep in the rain and the light, among the flowers
By the sanctuary of the walls, where no one comes,
And there is no more death and no more time –
And what is dead, and alive, are one

And by this font I want to be baptized:
To be born here, married here, die here, feast here –

This is the place of the heart's wild baptism,
The heart's own, its own way

Baptism, and faith in the broken –
Faith, broken the heart's way to resurrection;
There is no service here, no solemn congregation
Baptism, among the bees and the trees for witness

Baptism, and you touch me on my forehead
Baptism of touch, with all that matters most
Baptism, and he bows and cannot speak

Baptism of fire and of blood – and it's all beauty,
All of it, every fallen stone – none of it wasted –
None of it, ever

If you come here, come in your heart: only that

– in the rain
                    turning away
                                        to find you, now –

In the rain, out on the road to Dalmally
Past the old green road where he drove his sheep

– a thin green line
                              among the black dots …
gone back
              to ground – back into the dream –

Rob Roy, and you, Landless MacGregor –
Hounded by Grey Campbell and his Black Son

From Kilchurn to Glenstrae, into a ghost; and now?
Where the site is unmarked, and the name a river
By a farm gate and a cattle grid –

Where the road becomes sharp uneven fragments
We come, as slowly, to it: there

Under the mountain with its head of cloud,
Through staves of downward telephone wire,
Its scattered stones, covered like a scree slope;
The foundation, stretched into a mound
You have to guess at –

But it stands in the air, where it was;
It stands where air is stronger than stone
Grey, within grey, where the pass goes upwards
Grey as the rain-sky echoes its aura
Of in-seen, magnetic space

And this stone, smaller than a pebble,
With its bloodstain like a smear of quartz
Is red, is fresh – for you
                remembering

The Arrow of Glenlyon, fallen –
The house of love, beaten down

And Kilchurn, beside it, like a mere decoration
Smiling, cracked – empty. Justice.

The way the earth does it.

And the heart is a single swallow
Dipping and curving over the lake shore
Through the dusk
            in its arc –
its black-fork
            -tailed, sweeping flight
(catching midges!)

He flies alone and untrammelled
                 as if for us

He flies, unheeding
            faster than you can name him

Soft, to his word –
         and, one by one … seven come join him

And then those ducks, swimming along,
Come round from the island –
With one trailing behind

All at once, comically, dipping down;
Under the water, for what seemed
Far too long
        surfacing
                together, fifty yards on

Under the one sky
            that is cloud and loch
Cloud-loch, loch-space: containing us,
To see things, seeing them as they are
At the speed they are
            and of one, walking

(And to see why
          – or how –
The lightness is everything).

6

Before you wake –
Though the wind has blown all night,
Before you wake
I would bring you this peace.

Rest now. Be with your dreams.
For the road is long,
But I know the way.

I go alone now. I have come.
To this place of the heart again:

And the peace is everywhere, you can hear it now
The peace is the bees, the peace is the flowers,
The peace is the flies, the peace is the stones,
And the peace is the man, sitting there

With the stream flow, below, beneath the conifers
And what was rain ... become clear, become sun
And the rain's whisper, a slow sea in the trees
Breathing now, as a fly lands on the page

And rubs its antennae, as if trusting him
The way the bee trusts the thistle it nestles in,
And the tiny snail the wall it crawls across,
And the toadstools the moss stump they grow on

And the far wall leans in the arms of the tree,
The green world is given sanctuary
As I would give it to you –

And the font is a well of soul,
A deep black well of soul,
Bubbling up from inside like a fountain
To bathe your face in;

And as you kneel at last, and see it,
A voice like your own, but not your own,
Can tell you
                    Be cleansed in your heart.

And how long you were there, you don't know.
It seems you have been out of time.

It seems, it all seems, until you come to
And your foot half-trips over a heart-shaped stone:
I will carry it to you

Where you sit,
Lying as you woke in your cocoon
And you did not know who spoke to you,
But words came, and you wrote them, all of them

And the whole thing flowed from end to end:

She said *The way to the Goddess is steep*
And many have gone down without returning
But you shall

And the world is full of the prophesies of doom;
It is time for the prophecy of joy.
Speak it –

And know that the wounds within you
Are as nothing compared with your inheritance,
Child.

The way of the crucifixion is gone,
The time of joy and manifesting is at hand
And the way of the earth is the way of God:

You will be heard in all places by what you do;
Let your soul carry you
Let the spirit empty into you

And she ran, she ran out of the castle –
Holding a baby under her left arm
And a knife in her hand,
Stabbing at the invading men –

Black hair, and cloak – her eyes blazing
And the stone cleft she went under then,
Holding the child as she looked at her eyes
So still and blue in their calm

And her man gone, only the cave remaining,
The cave in the hill of her conceiving

Annie MacGregor, your sister and friend

The great silent vista of loch water
Shimmering behind you, and behind the tent –

– the silent stretches of conifers

                              and even more silent

the mountains, beyond –

As you sit on an upturned bowl,
In your kerchief; hardly believing,
Even, disbelieving

How it comes so out of time and place
To find us so unexpectedly in place
And what opens in us to meet it we have never seen

Praise be the fruit and the lion
Praise be in the days of fire to come
Praise be the one who sings this song

It is not courage or valour, but tenderness;
It is not loud – it is not arrogance
And it is stronger than steel: it is the rose

Marrow of wisdom, born from the rock

And if you want to hit the rock with the stone
Don't try to throw the stone at the rock
But let the stone
                  hit the rock

And he said, now I have come here at last, again

Think of all the ways the heart needs cleansing
For this new birth to take place –
It is not enough that the mind is made light;
The heart too must be made light

All mind-work now needs to be heart-work:
And this is the new education of earth.
For too long spirit has been understood in mind,
And this is why He came to earth

To show you the way of the heart
To show you that the way of heaven is earth's.
When you understand this, your lives will be released
In ways almost inconceivable to you now.

This wild place speaks it –
Fallen stones and rising ground –
And the font where heaven and earth meet, and in you.
And this is the task of speech:

To be of the heart, to be of your whole body,
That the heart alone can hold and contain
Every level within you – become mind in heart,
And heart in mind, though you have no word for it

No word for what the mind is to become.
And this is the place of fire –
To be brought into the heart and its cleansing,
And the meaning of birth and the heart are the same:

The heart is incarnation. It never forgets.
What it has lived, it always remembers … rose.
The soul-mind comes closest.

So in this place of prayer and peace
Let your prayers be for the heart of the people,
For the heart beyond all barriers and barricades,
And the fear of the mind and its defences.

Pray that the walls may fall as they are falling,
Now the wind is blowing – and remember

That the heart's way is resurrection:
To re-connect means the same.

Now go on your way and be glad
And know that to be a pilgrim is to walk

> *in the heart*

– for the heart.

This place is your beginning.

This place is our beginning and our ending.

Kilneuair, let no harm come to you:
Be sacred, be wild, be free.

Peace, and I would bring this to you:
Even this fragment of stone

And now it's time to go.

Buffeted in the night –
The tent flap shaken open, twice
(the elastic guys worn and gone)

Crouching on the sodden groundsheet,
And where the milk spilt – havoc.
The borderland is no place
                    to put roots down in.

The van packed, and the last of us
An oval patch of grass and flattened mud
Like a womb, or a mouth.

We leave no trace to the rain and the wind,
And the loch is quiet, the loch is hidden.

The road opens like a wet black ribbon,
On the edge of our unknown returning.

Loch Awe, Argyll and London

3

The Oak

for Richard Wainwright

THE OAK

Transcendent!
                    Beyond and above everything: every
season, every war, and the lightning that split and cleaved
you in two, rooting you (as far underground), and
wounding you:

but transcendent in this calm outreaching height of your
branches: calm, grown clear green and full in the blue
clouded air –

'I have outlived, I have outlasted myself'

Dragon tree, wounded tree, your arms spread like a silent
shout; and then a dancer, frozen in her gesture, alive,
breathing, silent, triumphant. Transcendent.

And you can see her eyes shining in leaf and sky

                              *

Now we come to you –
                    two women, and two men:
we closen with our eyes lifted in silence.

There is only the sound of our feet over the grass, and
our each seeing you, together and apart.

We only have eyes for you. Quietly, as we separate. Each a
tree

'I am each of your standing, and you are a part of me.'

                              *

What music, what
                        sheer melody there is in your upper
branches ... the deep note of a cello drawn once across its
strings, vibrating upwards –

and how *sad* and *touch* and *sleep* and *grace* are all in the
shape of them, and their curving beside each other.
Companion arms, as if ours, around each other.

But in you they are not apart, they have always been
together, from the whole being packed in your original
seed.

And yet surely not even that could have guessed what
you've lived and the things you have seen.

What an acorn: in solid gold bronze

'I have descended into the earth'

And now at your corner
                        where a huge fallen log lies,
adjacent, at the base of an angle it makes – your dead
shadow, with a fragment of hanging rusted chain lying
slack over it

as we pause to look down at it, and walk around its bleak
bark-stripped corpse

'I have shed my skins'

and this is your evidence –
and this is the shadow and the death you remember.
And it has no voice.

*

Rising

   rising now, as I stand under you gazing up
where one chain stretches, and the other is left
dangling … as the light dapples on your trunk like ribs,
speckling the bark and the thick green-lit leaves the blue
shows through

– and this is how far you have outgrown that moment,
now you stand like a Samson that has broken his chains
and pushed the pillars apart; and with no roof to crash
down because the roof is the sky.

You stand as you are, beyond recrimination – and that is
how large.

You could be telling me

'I stand as I am, and that is what I am'

      *

And you

   stand erect, and you stand proud … up the
sides of your trunk that part like flowing thighs a single
knob of wood like a shorn log rises out of, in the crevice,
free and bare out of its foreskin, and hard

'I am your Father'

– and you reach back your head and your arms behind
you, out of the picture

– and between your thighs at the knees, under your
covered sac, in the dark, is her womb cave opening:

      *

I have to breathe
                    I have to look aside … there at your
gnarled edges that cover the spire of the distant church, as
I reach out my hand and lean into you, feeling the hard
warmth of your ancient skin –

as hard as rivers, and as hard as only the heart can be

and then, as I look down, there in the bark in a shallow
dip is a hole like a navel – no bigger than an elephant's
eye, as the bark around it begins to soften like skin

tinged with red rust stain and interlaced with cobweb…

'I am not what you think'

'I am not your mind'

And glancing back at the head of the snapped-off dead
trunk: it has an ear that could be a horn, a sleepy closed
eye, a nostril and a mouth – but whether it is a cow or a
lion or a deep sea fish I don't know, but it has swum and
sunk down and stopped, and it lies dreaming of life at the
foot of your cross

and I stand, alive, dreaming of life. And I feel so absurdly
light.

*

Monolith of dreaming shadow
                          steep, sheer-sided,
flanked with dry fungus: a vertical tusk of ivy embedded
in your body; elephant-white, grey wolf, and worm. You
contain the memory of all creatures. They flow in your
veins and bark. Living Tree, living wood, museum and
monument – but the bones you carry are not dust, they

move and breathe. It is only that they are still. It is only
that I have to be still. To remember them in myself, and
in every dreaming cell

'You only have to listen'

and feel. How you bring me to my body, like a standing
sea   standing alone

'Be my son'

And I am nothing, if not human. Nothing.

*

Climbing ...
        where you have been up already, brother,
in your jade green jacket.

I stood back watching you, balanced in one black shoe
on a knob of bark, with your other left hanging, leaning
forward into your arms

embracing it, embraced ... and as I reach up for a first-
time handhold I fall back.

'Let go to me. I will hold you.'

And you could be Her saying that, as I climb your body,
and as I did ... and then it blurs. Flesh, warmth, and the
rush of soothing milk –

and now it's a waking, now it's You.

There's only this single round knot to swing your left foot
up towards; and then a single crack in the wood above it
to the right, to wedge your fingers in. There is only one

way up, and you can't see it until you climb it. You've got to believe it, and then you're there.

No imagining, no room for the slightest doubt. And the heave is *yes, I am here.*

Go on!

– and in a flash, boy-flesh and bark are one, and together they make man

– my muscles tensed, rippling with breath to every fingertip and toe, and my eyes open. Done it.

*

At the lip, then
                    where the sunlight slides out above
the depths … and I come face to face with a crop of tiny
branches sprouting out of the bark, each one leaved, a
seed, a future tree.

Child-trees on the rising slope. And this was the crown of
thorns, and your crown of gorse, but they are laurel now;
and every thorn is a fresh thing, an oak in miniature.

So it is in the Kingdom. And you bow your head.

And ahead a thick branch gestures like a curving arm –
and the field is green with sun, the sky blue between
clouds, and rising, its blue darkening and strengthening.

And you bow your head
                    and over the lip – you open
down, gazing into the brown dark, hollow, where the
lightning entered and gouged you, hollow

all the way down to the bole, the base!

Under where the bark gives way to bare wood, stained,
rippling, and curving: and you are a secret cathedral, a
vault, a cave of wood, a well that is your source.

Red dry and wet-streaked walls, where the rain falls and
soaks in and drips, silently

Reddened dry rotting walls like blood, red and brown
blood, pocked with tiny worm holes, pocketed and
knotted

Ruddy brown, veined, scarred with all a heart can feel, and
with all it has felt. Oh Heart of Ages, not a rock now, but
this, and only this

        living standing

        beacon of blood –

and from deep down the pungent rising scent of leaf-loam
I breathe, and breathe, as I drink it in like a rose I would
always remember.

Because this is the heart of you, Father. Fill me.

Dark, to your depths, and then light – now light –
lightened down where the sun reaches in,

and still as you breathe out you can see your breath, and
still you can't see the bottom you can only sense it, and
you can't see the end.

'Pour your fire into me'

        *

Enough now
you seem to say: your heart beating like
a slow clock, ticking back into warmth. Warmth, and then
heat. Blood, pounding.

Time, time, in a world of time. We have only so long here,
and it is never enough. It is enough to be touched. Just
once. Once, and forever.

Pressed, pinned freely up against this tree –

and so you turn to jump down, hardly wondering how, as
you step, and jump back ... bending both your knees,
down.

*

'Now see how I am rooted'

– the breadth of your base not even a giant could
embrace, prostrate, lying flat on his face ...

It takes sixteen paces round.

But we could hold hands here, as if for a May Dance. And
we could be in black going counter to the clock.
Your heart has seen it all and it's no longer your concern.
You care only for one thing: wholeness. 'There is nothing
outside of God.' You could even have given Eckhart your
bark.

And at this side you lean like a greenwood tree for lovers.
A greenwood and a gate, for meeting and farewell.

You are a tree fit for a king to hide in, and become a child
again.

And you are a mighty sign and a wind to all the
governments of the world.

Rajas, and your feet are elephant's – your feet are all the
feet that have ever walked; and your feet are the poor, the
lame and the lonely, indented with sores, signatures, and
burrow holes.

Your roots are another kingdom, alive like the disc of the
moon in a rippling lake.

You house Creation mirrored there, teeming with birds
like black shadows in your underbranches – perching,
then flying, and landing again.

And I walk round, and I walk round, and there is no
ending only the beginning of your truth.

Because you are here, at the end, and you will be here
until the end. This is your time, and your final full
ripening.

*

And in the cloudy morning half-light, as I walk back
towards you, towards the field's hedge-fenced edge –
and stop short:

there, on the bare patch of earth that surrounds you, is
your guardian; standing squat in his horns, looking away
ahead in front, his nostrils exhaling misty air.

Upper Holcombe and Edge Farm, near Painswick, Gloucestershire

4

The Sacred Way

for Jane Routh and Martin Palmer
written for Sacred Britain

THE SACRED WAY (VIA SACRA)

1

Here, I said, here where you stand
And pause, and let everything go still
Feeling your breath as you glance down
Is the ground that is everywhere –

                nameless under our naming

As it ebbs to your feet like a sea
That your heart knows already, as it breathes
Out through the soles of your feet, with relief.

2 Temenos

Sacred, sacrosanct, sanctuary
In the ruins of what was sacred space that we need back

These monoliths to moon and sun remind us
That we abandoned the stars for ourselves, only to find
That we have no rite for being human

But now as the breeze stirs, and we slow our steps
Where stone breathes we can receive its whispered gift
    again.

3 The Well

Dig under:
Where the well is depth, is other
Is the underworld, the otherworld, the Earth's and Hers –
What do you want? What have you brought here?

And as the gold coin of your asking sinks like a sun
Into the slippery moist mirror of its blackness
You may find the Source, and the cure:
That to dry up is to die.

4 The Other City

Deep in sun-bright memory and longing
And around on the ground invisibly at our feet
Lies the Other City, that is home – glimpsed
In the light between our eyes that lifts our exile:
So we say: put the heart back where we live
In this Babylon of bondage: raise it to the sky
So we can feel a haven around us again –
Bring our city back to the Divine.

5

And outside, in the depth of a timeless wood
– where you drive under trees as sunlight dapples –
Is the green heart of magic, the other world
Where everything is written, alive in the silence
And you can become the unknown one you are again

The creature, the dreamer, the witness ... till you emerge

And you will not harm with eye or hand
And you will greet and grieve the wild ones as your
    friends.

6 The Green Road

There is a green road that runs
Through an ordinary but extraordinary garden
Where trees have been replanted
In clustered sheaths like candles

It is the Garden of the Earth

Once boots trod there and carts bumped
You can feel them in your stride
And hear the soundless accents of conversation

Now it is a tractor-mown path
Flanked by waist-high wild flowers
(Where you may disturb a sleepy owl)

Leading to a landslip above a tan-brown river
That has become a precipice of fragile ground

And there, beyond the river, it continues
Like a vein above the sheep-grazed grass
Where a little grove of trees has grown among its stones
As it snakes towards the rising hill under its ridge

And as you walk on its soft springy turf now
You can be a part of all your heart feels
And know that its threading blood-line is real

Human as you are, from your sky into your feet.

7 postcards for pilgrims

a

Start here (or anywhere you are) seeing
That to call this journey *pilgrimage*
Means an echoing in your heart
That changes it

Meaning who you are, too

Suddenly in your innermost unnamed self
That has always called itself you –
Being who you were always meant to be

b

And as you go, read the signs
What is gathering around you?
Everything is secretly written on air
To feed, sustain and awaken you

The journey is itself, and it is your eyes
And something vaster than us is speaking
Through the intricate text of Its Being
Beat by beat and breath for breath –

c

And as the journey grows
Weaving you in with your companions
Why these people? This motley bunch, seemingly random
But assured ... as boundaries soften

Bringing up all you need to see and feel, until
We are all One Body – straggling or smiling
We are messengers for each other, like a medicine
We are stories to be told and heard: a cargo of treasure.

8

What are these ruined shells? Shrine or castle
Where the sun warms or the wind blows –

What does it mean for us to remember
Injustice and power, beside true loving?

These stones speak for themselves: but we must read
    them
To see what our history could be again

As it hangs in the balance of our wakefulness
To stand up and be counted, to renew and mend

9

Soul that breaks the mould
That sees what a far-flung landscape is
And blends to it

That gets out and walks
The whole way to feel –
To witness the unforgettable

Heron-bird of life and death
And the light on the longed-for island raying down

10

And can see then
As the borderland becomes the Summerland
Where we are drawn into the light beyond:

Ascending light, like a dream within us
Dissolving the black ganglia that hang over Britain

In this sacred each and only moment
Where inner and outer are one

11 The Glory

Stand in the presence
Though you cannot name it
By any name, or only one

Stand in the presence
Where the bread is given
Stand and sing –
Where all our names are sung

Stand and see
At the harvest of time
That as we build in the light
Your Will shall be done

And in the temple between us
That is a ruin of light
That is a man and a woman
Made of naked light

As the veil is lifted –
We shall see the beginning
That lies hidden in the end

That we are all a part
Of each other, in ourselves
Everyone, everything, everywhere sacred
Living on this pilgrim star

Then we shall find each other
In the Glory.

5

Culbone

for all who walk here
for Jenny, Barrie, Lucy, Lara

and in memory of Joan

In its time of spiritual origin Culbone was created as a place of PEACE – a place where men could find rest for their physical beings and stillness for their bodies. This power of PEACE was built into the ground, the rocks, the trees and into all vegetation. PEACE is the vibration of an actual spiritual substance.

Joan Cooper, Culbone: a spiritual history

Culbone is a very special place and it is also one of those 'anonymous places of the spirit'. You can find it easily enough if you want to off the A39 high on Exmoor's edge beyond Porlock Hill. Turn right at the Culbone Inn and follow signs for Ash Farm (where Coleridge wrote 'Kubla Khan' in an opium-induced reverie in 1798) and Silcombe Farm till you arrive in a small grass lay-by fifty yards up from a five-bar wooden gate that has the church service sheet pinned to it. Coleridge's 'deep romantic chasm' points to Culbone Valley just below Ash Farm.

Mostly ramblers find the place. From the gate on, you become one of them, walking a level then descending stony path; the sea still visible ahead of you to the South Wales coast before you come to the edge of the wood. From there you can either turn right in among the trees or go straight on. Either way, the walk and the silence is preparation for what lies beneath in the valley's depth, high as it still is, hundreds of feet above the sea.

With its tiny ninth-century church dedicated to the Welsh St Beuno, Culbone is truly a place of peace, as Joan D'Arcy Cooper, an American who lived at Culbone Lodge for thirty years until her death in 1982, recognized and named in her writing. Joan, a Christian mystic and clairvoyant, was both a remarkable teacher and spiritual healer. She recognized (as Barry O'Connor, its present owner, emphatically does) that the place *itself* is a healer, both overtly and discreetly. It is also a place to be simple as well as grounded, to let go of the things you don't need. It is a place to receive.

Culbone is both light and dark; it remembers its past. In its long history it has also been a place of suffering as well as poverty. And after dark on a very cloudy night it can be so black you can barely see your hand in front of your face. It is one of the so-called 'dark spots'; correspondingly, the stars you can see when the sky is clear are scintillating in their multitude, a great spray curving above the treetops into infinity.

I first came to Culbone in 1992. It has stayed with me ever since — as it has with many, as the visitor's book in the church continually testifies. Thousands have been here and have been touched by its spirit, with or without words. It is a fragment of unspoilt earth (too precipitous to have ever been cultivated), and a self-preserving portal, or entry-point of heightened energy, which is said to be particularly strong on the 'Lovelace Seat' at the top corner of the churchyard.

And the picturesque church is only a part of it. What surrounds it invisibly, which Joan believed was imprinted from the beginning, may also remind us that 'everywhere is sacred'. The rest is for each of us to discover, and in our own being. *A centre under the world that holds.*

CULBONE STONE

Three feet high in a glade of faery pines
grey and moss-covered – and lined
with an unmistakeable grin seen from the side,
a Puckish Pan face in the permanence of stone
(to lighten up a dull day, who knows)
supplanted by a sign: gouged near the top
an encircled cross, laid like Jesus stumbling
the long piece pointing down
from this high ground, to the hidden valley below

piercing its ear, and as your eyes re-align
it becomes a gravestone: but marking who, what, when?
A change as radical as it became betrayed,
a ritual in the mists we can only imagine
become future, for us standing here now
in this extraordinary blue November morning,
bent, tracing our fingers in its rain-smoothed shape,
for our own journey of remembering

under the world, and out of time.

A MOMENT INSIDE

A veil as light as mist
as if kissing the eyes

Everything heavy lifted
washed down by the foaming winter streams

Gossamer cobweb gathering
around a white shrouded face

Here in this privileged pew
where anyone can become it

Your mind lifted into peace
into the after-rain silver light of peace

and the air and earth smell you're breathing
the roaring muffled water whispering

eyes closed in this momentary dream
a shaft of silence between the sounds

of all our jarring shadows

ONLY LISTEN

Imagine what might happen
if you shut your mouth and listened:

you might fall into a thousand
pieces of light

each irradiated
with birdsong and blue sky

each of them speaking
your original name.

In all your senses –
hearing, tasting,
touching, smelling, and sensing –
fill them with listening

and you will find yourself again.

*

And when you have become your listening
your breath will heal you of all misgiving

and all the tightness you have held
all over your body and being

will become a babbling stream of healing,
caressing and soothing, sustaining every cell …

and you will be the one you always were within,
who silently lives underneath everything.

*

And if you listen, high above the sound of the water
in the sun-dappled beech trees like a church built
all around the birdsong – you may hear

a flute: dipping, and gliding, and soaring
in and out of the stillness of a dream ...

And long after the girl who played the flute has gone
you will hear, or imagine you hear, her song ...

half-heard between the leaf-breeze and the stream
where it has become your listening.

THE INVITATION

In the church at the bottom of the world
where there has been church for a thousand years
is the silence at the depth of your body,
deepening like a shelf reaching under your heart
where the densely wooded valley slopes outside
and steepens: uninhabited, unspoilt, unpolluted
as you walk on its high paths above the dreaming sea
sheltered by the leaves' green canopy like an animal …

And where the stars shine as you've never seen them
white-clear as pinheads, clustered thick as trees
with the white dust of galaxies beyond, between them,
so that the universe itself seems a different place
as you lean back against a gravestone, gazing;

And now the morning birdsong tells you the same –
we are part of a timeless Creation if we know our place
and its gateway and ground is PEACE, as you proclaimed.

Come to the church at the bottom of the world
'through caverns measureless to man …'
where the sun of the world hangs, at midnight
come back to the beginning: breathe, surrender, see.

PRELUDE

Unimaginable temple
conduit of energy
like the stream pervading
from just above your crown –
streaming through you, as you sit now
settling and soothing behind your eyes,
emptying your mind
to present warmth
into the valley of peace
surrounding your heart

Unimaginable temple
wholly physically present
only guessed at in shafts of sunlight
glancing obliquely across you ...
such is the work of heaven
beyond our imagination,
only mimicked in forms
like Ionian columns
crested in gold.

Stasis of earth, stability of centuries,
fluidity of heaven, the countless dreams of angels
and the two circling inside us
like an uncertain caduceus –

two lovers only sure
of each other's otherness.

Peace the only certainty here,
their fusion together
two hands moulding clay
for the place to be called by its names.

Peace that is stronger than anger, or circumstance,
peace that is stronger than love, even,
until you realize love's reality ...

Peace that is shedding
all we bring, to simplicity,
the letting go of everything
that is inessential:
possessions, words, gestures

and all the other toys
of disconnected fantasy.

When you let go of everything
then you will know peace
that is the light of the world.

And live together?
Her dream, and ours
a temple surrounded by huts,
a church fringed by cottages,
a centre, and a dwelling place.

So many different gatherings
of the chosen and the outcast
masters and slaves
of one unrealized race
extended on the long journey
of evolution through time –
the only reason for being here.

There is so much we can do together
we can never achieve alone,
and still our aloneness
is the point of Self

point and portal
residing in each one of us
that intensifies the whole.

And still neighbour does not meet neighbour
while the walls of ego are in place;
only a heart broken by transparency
can dare to let the other in
seeing the truth that we are One.
Tourist and T'ai Chi master alike
disciples, and slaves of rest,
all craving the same ground,
all silenced by the same fear

of ceasing to exist in a greater light,
when all we can finally do is die.

And all the rest takes time
stretching a luminous canvas
beyond these temporary shadows,
imprinting atoms that radiate
into rock, tree, leaf and stream.

Peace, the substance, the vibration of peace.

Slowly, slowly the coming
of the knowing of peace.

Its end our only end, and beginning.

ACCORDING TO THE PLACE

> Varied spiritual levels have continued to exist
> contemporaneously in Culbone, representing nearly
> six thousand years of human history
> > *Joan Cooper*, Culbone: a spiritual history

i

Came the sage
with his invisible face
to this densely wooded place
(was there even a clearing?)

from what is now the sea.
Came to teach men
how to find a voice within,
the beginning of individuality.

Beyond dogma: revelation of what is
(as it was in the beginning)
self-evident, unesoteric, even

and so he called the place Kashebah
meaning 'the spirit is at work'.

To all who came: this knowledge
of how to listen from within
each according to his own –

beyond the tribe outside
that was the world, and still is.

The sage's pupil continued this,
both of them here for fifty years
and then for 750 years, nothing.

And nothing was built in stone.

ii

Woodsmen, primitive, passing through,
living here for shelter

and leaving nothing.

And for 750 years, again nothing,
only the trees
and the memory of their shadows
in the rustling of squirrels
on last year's leaves

and a thin track over the sloping shore.

iii

Came seven men
(one teacher, six students)
from the West of Britain centre
remembering the golden age
of fifteen hundred years before.

The memories that never leave us
until we achieve them again?

And now, a small community
of smoking fires among the trees
with folk coming from far and wide ...

as they still come,
unrealized in peace.

And each man lived for his inner teacher
that became the angel
he would himself one day become.

iv

No building remains
but: six pieces of jade stone
hand-carved with a symbol
scattered around the churchyard
still waiting to be found
in the shade of the yew.

Six essential runes.
I sleep, I eat, I breathe, I love you,
I make love with you
and *we belong to God in peace.*

v

One ailing teacher left
trapped by mortal limitation
having to surrender to his reluctant family
moving into the unoccupied huts.

The human drama submits to longevity
ache, and the absence of a summit
in the mystery of why we live as we do.

Still they clung to his memory
for as long as they could …

vi

Pushed out by a tribe of forty
with a lot less manners –
(their shouts still echoing in the valley)

The woodsmen, returning,
evolved into early farmers
living in caves near the sea.

Another five hundred years of simplicity.
And when they left, 130 years
for the place to breathe.

Even places need to be left alone.

vii

Came another man
also needing to be left alone
without anything
but his inner prompting
the secret task of his life

the healing of everything
that had accumulated here
eclipsing the Original Peace.

He was the first priest.

His work, for three decades
his testament, the first building in stone.

To be as strong as anything
you need to be stronger.

viii

And then again the locals moved in,
evolved into building and farming
(the alternating rhythm continuing
woven like strands of a braid ...)

Heaven followed by earth,
horizontal after the vertical
each levelling the other –

each mysteriously intersecting
in what would become the cross.

ix

And then for nearly a thousand years
nothing but cave dwellers.

A sigh in the wind, in your mind.
The earth's ineffable patience

everyone and everything
part of the process.

x

And then again a solitary man
came and built a hut in stone
continuing where the first priest was,
his task also to cleanse,
where outside and inside are one
and can be One again.

Baptist to a teacher
who was himself a Baptist
to a great light's coming
speaking to all those who came

of the New that was on its way
seen by both men from within, like a sun.

A radiant figure in the light
before incarnation, and beyond it
out of the mysterious, all-powerful sun

and within
through the heart's shining ...

xi

Can you imagine Him here?
Standing among the trees
in the clearing
in the Village of Man and Woman

laying on his hands,
the longed-for
healer and lover,
Beloved

Son, sun, lunar,
the first
complete human.

We saw a great light
and it irradiated our minds
thrilling in our blood
haunting us with all
we were created to be

that only now
could we begin to receive.

Caritas, agape
the most intimate
eros of the heart's true being

planted in each of us like a seed.

And then He built the foundation
for the Temple of Light
high in the air
higher than the church
higher and higher
forever undefiled
so it could descend as healing
for Jew and Gentile
and never be claimed
by any and all
who would come to betray Him
in His name.

xii

From flame to flame to inner flame
three generations, and 170 years
the chain of light unbroken –

And then, as Caesar's Rome went on
in its crepuscular journey of awakening,
the woodsmen returned, for as long.

And Constantine gave way to Nero
as the city burned, for a song.

Came seven monks from Wales, by boat,
closening up the track from the sea
with their mission

re-naming the place: Kitnor
after the cave, and clearing it
to begin again. Six cells and a centre
where eating, study, and prayer all took place.

No separate chapel

no hierarchy, or binding Rule;
they held all things in common
and remembered His solitude.

And what it is in you
that yearns to be like them,
although you don't know their name
(lost in the Celtic mists of time),
is what drives you inwardly now
although you can't explain
how the inner and outer monk divides.

And just in this way
the mystery teaching was lost
and church replaced divine inner knowing
superior to its source, materialized

in the culture that called itself Christ.

(And so the chain of light was broken.)

xiii

Two lights: a carved stone window
with a worn column between them
and a boar's head beneath –

the woods rumbling with them then.

The woodsmen moved in again
where the monks had been,
thirty of them, living their own green lives

also according to the place.

And then for seventy-five years again nothing
but the stream, the leaves, and the birdsong

that are always here in the pauses
before the bridge fills with visitors again
half-glimpsed through the hazel's protection ...

xiv

And in the year Columba landed on Iona
they wanted to build a kirk here.

Eighteen and a half long, by ten and a half wide
with its thatched roof, no bigger than a barn
and subject to the same cycles as its setting.

How could it be otherwise?
Priests wandered in and out
sometimes alone, or bringing their flock

and then mostly the building was alone
as it is now, somewhere between
Christ and deep water

the valley's continual song.

When the monks were murdered on the Strand
it burnt down in one to the ground
and for a century remained a ruin to the rain.

Rebuilt with only the foundation,
the two lights, and some of the charred timbers,
enlarged with a porch, and thatched again.

Around 1090, abandoned to the rain
and the age's darkness outside

the thatch leaking through – the walls
left slowly liquefying
the way only stone knows
about its yearning for water.

xv

Deserted, the place breathing
its own deep rhythm ...

What else is there? Layers above,
the sudden interruption of radio
leaking from a house
playing schmaltzy music
(a sign of how far we have come).

But then Kitnor became a home
to those outcast and on the edge –
the banished children of imagination

left to their own devices,
dumped by an embarrassed clergy
with even their own church in ruins
locked up in the living air.

It's hard to imagine
how they fended for themselves
making the church a shelter,
only later building their own.

It was Culbone's first community,
a place without a priest –
but a home for the presence of love
and what love needs.

Forty good years
where neighbour loved neighbour
striving for understanding
(how shamed the visiting curate
must have been ...)

Lived, died, and buried here,
their being still in the inner air
like voices half-heard in the stream
when the dark is deepest.

xvi

1305: church rebuilt for the third time
once the nuisances had gone.

Church powerful throughout the land;
Kitnor one of many 'projects'.

Local labour paid for by tithes
extracted from working people.

Once again, the same foundation
and the charred beams carried over,
enlarged again slightly in size
(puffing its medieval chest)

and still the priest was often
the only one present
surrounded by the spirits of the dead.

xvii

Imagine being imprisoned here
on a sunny afternoon
in this place of peace
(who would want to leave anyway?).

Theft or adultery
a few months or years;
however, it was Men Only
(the whole wooded declivity
their only deepening Mother).

Allowed to bring nothing
but the clothes they stood in –
then sentenced to Coventry

only forced to attend church services
for their better instruction.

Separated from their families,
nothing to do day or night,
some crazed into suicide.

Their judges' crime
to make this place a living hell
sanctified by righteousness.

It has not been forgotten.

Ninety-three years of this, and then
(you guessed it –)
the place becomes uninhabited

the church itself derelict until after
the dissolution of the monasteries.

xviii

Nowhere else to put them,
nothing we can do for them,
so send them to Kitnor.

And so the lepers came.
And no one gave them anything:
sentenced to themselves.

This second community
founded on the church of the first:
the real church of humanity
and caring that the Master taught.

And so they cared for each other
as simply as breath
in the love that moves in our hearts
when all else fails.

A slit in a thick stone wall
that you may sit beside today –
while they rebuilt the church once again.
(The so-called 'leper's window'.)

And the hermit priest
hid from their suffering,
a crab in his own little world;

while his spurned flock watched the services
through the three eye-level windows
and never received communion.

xix

Adam and Eve
naked in the valley
with a tree and apples ...

covered in lime whitewash now
the truth of our nakedness
in this garden before God.

But it hums in the valley
and streams in our veins
while we make love in the morning ...

And for nearly a century, nothing
after Shakespeare and the last leper died.

And still the priest officiated alone
keeping his tiny flame of reason alive.
(Who knows what passed through his mind?)

xx

The third community came:
a group of Somerset families
who knew how life could be
and wanted to live it.

A world within a world
already long gone wrong.
They brought it all with them
to begin it over again.

Prayed and worked together,
home-educated their children,
created their own entertainment
as simply as the baking of bread.

xxi

You found their crude dwellings
among the rhododendrons –
thirty-eight East Indian servants

sent to work as charcoal burners
for twenty-one years, for their freedom.
And again no women with them.

They were the fifth community
defined by the shadow of their skin
(and by how we treated them).

Small boats appearing in the cove
to take their charred produce
in exchange for tea and sugar.

And they were not happy here,
far from their home and longing.

They made the church their centre,
attended it, and mended the roof
needing no priest either.

He had comfortably long escaped,
leaving them to their natural fate
as the valley gave them all she could.

xxii

Local men moved in again
using their foundations –
the trees thick with billowing smoke,
the whole place become a smithy.

Four to a kiln, two at a time,
two away collecting wood –
the kilns going day and night
sweating hell-fire heat.

One-room stone huts their signature
living rough in the woods,
riggers away from their families,
monks without God.

And in the same year Shelley drowned
their fires burnt out …
and still the sea was dreaming
through the leaves of beech and ash.

xxiii

Four families moved in;
you could call them squatters,
the ownership here still undefined
till the landlord made them tithed –
but they were still free to do their own thing.

The church remained a ruin
till the Wesley virus swept the West:
this time the roof was slated

the Ash family private pew added,
and the hermit cell dismantled,
its doorway sealed shut.

The priest would never again be
apart from his people.

And outside, the market cross set up
brought in scores of bright faces,
their produce guaranteed and blessed
like their merriment afterwards.

This was Christian Culbone at its best.

Even one of the cottages became an inn
selling simple homemade beer
for traffic off the packhorse track.

And still the shadow waited
in the higher world above …

xxiv

Private ownership: estate management
tied cottages, giving everything they had
to those in control safely removed
(their seat a folly called Ashley Coombe
wired among bitter rhododendrons now)

And the open-air markets fell silent.

When cottage owners died
their homes went to outsiders

vetted and chosen by the Estate.
The lodge became a gamekeeper's dive.

What else are Capitalist entrepreneurs
but gods without God?

And so a hamlet became a memory,
and a prophecy of the life to come.

XXV

1897: and still building the church
where a living church has no end.
Windows, roof woodwork, and reredos.
Rood screen, family pew, and font,
a belltower and a harmonium
for the century to come

even as the valley breathes in its own time
as it always has, and shall;
one part light, the other in shadow
(as a red arrow tears the sky −)
as twilight stirs the past, and beneath
a mystery as deep as its stream channel
reaching among fallen trees to the sea.

Twilight, when those still bound here
breathe in the memory of their own air
as one bright woman works to give them peace.
Two thousand souls, one for each year
we have come from Golgotha −
the slaves and us, their masters
caught in the same borderland
filling the uneasy stillness ...

borne one by one towards the light.

The same woman who lies buried here
caught by cancer in her prime
full of a love that goes beyond time
who understood the dreaming, forever lingering
in her after-echo, and three wooden huts.

Priests may come who understand this
and this story – meanwhile the place
goes on in its own journey
deeper than any theory,
into the core of each dreamer.

'If you must tell them anything
tell them Only Listen —'
you finally heard it said as you asked.

xxvi

And if you sit here where she suggested
in front of a grey memorial wall,
its carved letters blurred by black lichen

you may feel and see that invisible sun,
its heat rising as if from the ground
inexplicably warm and bright, and you may know
what it means to be gentle and alive
where your heart is neither troubled nor afraid
above the gravestones leaning up like tongues

because you're free to listen as you are
being no one but yourself, as you breathe
becoming the stillness where love is peace.

6

The Mountain

for Mary

Believe in the peak 'entrance to the deep secret'

The Ox and His Herdsman *(trans. M.H. Trevor)*

To climb finally at last above everything.

Black gold sunset sky
the valley darkening with its lights,
winter trees silhouetted on the inky ridge
as I turn to the open field's height

and an owl calling

       just now

into the darkness

      into the light

Finally I turn.

Ahead, in a still undarkened blue sky
Venus shining, its light refracted
like a large leggy mosquito drifting ...

with the kiss of life.

call of the mountain

i

In the beginning, you don't even see it.
Its outline invisible, voice mute as yours
locked in where you are
in what you call your life.

It begins as a longing
to take a long drive in the rain
any way out, away
my soul needs to breathe
you never thought you'd hear yourself say it.

And here you are on your way
towards someone or something you'd never
quite dared face
and when it comes to it, you can't wait.

The call of the mountain in the rain.

ii

Away, towards, at last, leaving
and you're driving into a mirror
of your impatience and irritation
at the car in front of you –

of your littleness, the very size
you are being called beyond.
You see it?

The wipers keep working
to make your vision clean

so there's nothing but you

and air between.

iii

You sit in the Hereford eco-cafe
full of delightfully vain useless objects
and read about her tragic assassination.

Wheels within wheels
of rhetoric and reprise
and living by the sword
become her sacrifice.

How see it from the mountain's eye?

iv

Out on the old road of longing
with all its signs

the bridge over the old brown bull town
the chocolate factory with its puce green towers
the mysterious tree-lined avenue
with its floating cotton-wool blossom
suspended like time.

Ten summers, and the road
never arriving

always its promise deferred

until you realize
it was all in your mind

and longing alone
can never reach its own end

the journey, its own demise

the call beyond, and beyond
what you think it will be

her eyes, her lips, her naked body.

v

Tunnel of rain, mile after mile
as the land rises over the border
into mountain country
its silence and expanse.

Its presence all around despite
and later in the fading light.

Persevere, you tell your knight
and then the brief respite of blue sky
cloud lifting like smoke –
the green of the fields returned
before the grey returns

Wilder. Worse
the slicks of water thickening by the road
past the occasional chapel

low grey stone walls

becoming moorland, with rivers
barely contained in their banks
in blasting cold wind

World's winter, alternating
ten centuries ago for the Wanderer
now motorized ...

                      only

and as unexpectedly as the journey dictates
raindrops drifting towards the headlights
falling like a rain of light
at the darkest time ...

shadows of the mountains shouldering out
of the rain mist like whales
giant and awake.

vi

Arriving on the flat plain
at what she says is *the end of the world*
a harbour facing the winter sea in the mist.
The ferry poised, spectral; the streets
empty but for ear-chilling wind ...

A lone driver in a jet black car
reflecting blue light below as it moves
with nowhere to go, passing by twice –

Her flat like a white cube above it all
the shouts and lingering voices past midnight
and hers resonant with the one thing she says
that is already climbing
(as you glance at me aside)

*You know, love is something we all need to do
and it's not even personal ...*

as I turn and turn in the night.

being on the mountain
(two mountains)

1

A workhouse at its base
brick walls with intricate grille windows
beneath a vertical chimney
hollowed, abandoned now
but for summer visitors
but not here today as the wind blows.

Poor house is where it starts
to climb above poverty and labour
for your life, for the right to be
without having to be a lifeless doing.
The steps are easy – and for some
they are chillingly void and empty.

One way up. She talks about sex
a previous partner impotent
what women and men need to hear
about each other, this Book of Air ...
voices across a divide in a final great listening.
And the root is, neither of us can do it
without our ground.

Sex falls away, and what is there
a whole new conversation
called *heartspring*
feeling in to all it could now be.

And as the wind wraps our faces
near-shouting to make ourselves heard
turning

Nothing here. These bone white outcrops.
Then the sun.

All the world that's left below
houses, harbour, ferry, shipwreck sea
waves' white spray leaping over the cobb wall

abandoned as Jesus
in his final mortal hour

abandoned as we are
to the world of time

where all we have
is our standing, I.

---

interludes

Sometimes you just need black space
to rest your overheated mind
the whole created world cancelled
from white, and its consciousness.

So in these bare white walls I find
a blackness within, turning out the lights
to enter non-being, to be
the One I can surrender to – Life.

*

But your vision has to be dragged through the mud
to be tested ... she's saying
and suddenly two, three years' mud is clear
as a terrible fire you walk into
where everything precious you have
is burning around you –

until all you have is the knowledge
that all you thought you had

was its shadow.

*

'The path is pleasant, joyful and familiar'
I remind you, Eckhart to your St John
on this beautiful winter lawn by the sea
weaving in between coves, and along.

It's true we shouldn't have to struggle:
if we had the courage to be really natural
we'd walk this way all of the time
without even needing to call it heaven.

2

The path leads way up above the small town
gathered to its height, higher
than building has ever been:
fields, stone walls, grass, moorland, then mountain.

Up through a farm gate, an eager collie
abandons his territorial persona
then re-assumes it for the sake of duty.

A thread of pouring rainwater greets us
on the other side, a river as we climb
— pure flow, and overflow —
towards the old Roman trackway
the old grey path of slavery.

And you are bound to your work on broken estates
the after-Christmas rubbish blowing
among mindsets that drag at you and drain you
in a crucifixion of loving.
And we must go on loving
our only promise – I
putting our arms around you.

Another town far below
looks quite different from this side
bordering a promontory island behind us;
the majesty of the land has become all estuary
mountain, moorland, fields, houses, sea

You can breathe.
And you enter the old stone circle.

Sitting huddled against one
standing like a cloak around us
we talk and laugh over our modest picnic
with no other care in this world
until the wind says it's time to go

and bear the mountain's gift down.

*

for T.

Is it how you sit
large hands in your lap, poised
slightly straight-backed
blond-greying hair tied up now
still more deeply yourself, and your age
your voice settled, and as female
as anyone could be?

... just trying to live seamlessly, as you say
quietly, listening before you speak
your always considered verdict
timelessly from within

despite the years, despite everything

and is this what it means
to be in your mountain?

*

How does it seem from the mountain?
When fever or grief takes you ...
your teachers have been Love and Death
your journey huge as this landscape.

Never just what it literally seemed
for you, or anyone: we are all symbolic
messengers for each other
in an invisible temple we can barely see

for rain or tears, though it's always here
as we move in and out of each other's lives
at the unprepared-for appointed time
as we live, and as we die ...

And there's a third place beyond either
you have no name for –
you are being called to
that some call the Self, that has no home.

*

They call this place the Pilgrim Hotel.
You can just drop in for a cup of tea.
You've driven all day in the silence to discover
that everything is exactly as it should be.

staying on the mountain

i

Spacious, broad, expanded – imagine
as the mountain is in your standing
like Leonardo's man

not pulled back into reaction
at the first thing she says to you
or seduced by her reality
suffused in dismissive anger –

the test you fail, to rise again
and keep rising until you stand
where I and the Father are one.

ii.

for D.

When romance dies and real is all there is
after all these years, what's left between?
And yet it can be still like meeting
for the first time, where everything is fresh
as it should be, the heart gathering no dust

The blue of the sky above the winter trees climbing
the path reaching on across the fields
beyond where you've so far been ...

And finally the view down
the spire through the mist become blue
at the blinking of an eye: grey to blue
and back again, and again blue
– the air's transparent rune –
before you descend, in the given time.

iii

'If she was to die now,
then what would you most miss about her?'
The question that brings the whole mountain

                                 back into view

as wide as your open mouth …

iv

Your longing so easily transferred
look how it can move from one woman to another
with such indifferent ease.

What does it mean for that hungry ghost
to return home to you, to give
his shivering need-driven body
shelter and more than shelter
the warmth of a body, *your* body
in *your* incarnation?

That is your work.
You don't even need to call it a marriage
though it is one, with the one
who's closest to you
who you so strangely grow to love
as you would a once dubious stranger:
you here in the house of winter.

And whoever you're drawn to
feeling the anchor
of this holding:
you in harbour
among all the other boats
floating in the blackness
of the Night Sea full of dreaming stars.

V

for Henry

As the details of our meeting fall away
and fade into their laughing embrace
that takes the Sunday News with it
as you say *beyond the littleness, we are it!*

The Self. All of us
all one, all from the mountain, forgotten
and as deeply buried within
under all the layers of our disbelieving
'The person of no rank constantly
going in and out of the face ...'

The pure, true, free one
the one who means it (and is)
and when we come to our father's house
we come for him.

Your father and mine
and the true father calling
in this kiss of the invisible
on top of your crown
woken as you are.

And when we can love the wreckage
in this one and only
amor fati

as we laugh another kind of laugh.

vi

There is a break between emotion
and this mountain air: a gap in logic
in all that is reasonable, or seemingly
before we get near

to where we really are, or why
this has happened
this latest catastrophe of loving
as you tell your restaurant story

and after an hour of mountain roads
French highways in choked silence
it's you now catching a glimpse of yourself
in the mirror – suddenly hearing yourself say
it's OK, Debbie, it's OK

with a gentleness and compassion for yourself
you've never known –
only outwardly for those you've held
come home now, come to this

and a few minutes later, for the first time,
you cry.

vii

All it is imagined
in all you can say
(in the wellness of our faces
people can as easily mistake)
in the paring down
the density goes

and in this time
where one you've loved as well
has become a hating enemy
all that's left: dignity, like a moat
round a fortress of being

as much to keep us in
as shield them out –
to keep us on our mountain
standing in terra firma

surrounded by a softening
circle of water

and no visible armour
only eyes and air
a naked suit of air.

viii

What does it mean for your heart
to stay on the mountain?

To remain in love
not stoop to the low shooting
of your gut

or even deeper the revenge
of the place of black water

all the way down
to root numb.

Hatred is very grounding you once said
and only love gets us unstuck again –

the choice to live
below or above

to return to the heart's silence
knowing its speech in love.

ix

To stay with the slow nectar of yourself
and not be tempted out
unless the door inside opens

or that cat, sitting waiting
at the bottom of the telegraph pole
where a squirrel is trapped, gazing down
needs some divine intervention.

Everywhere, everything interweaving
seen and unseen. The reasons
slipping away under the river
black eels thrashing, now vanished …

and why we couldn't stay together.

All there is, the peace
and this place of returning
that is the heart's mountain

bathed in transfigured light.

x

Heat of anger
hardening of heart, harsh
as you sit in the aftermath.

You ask for forgiveness
for that part of it
and a voice as clear
as another's in your ear says

Forgive yourself.

You turn back in
and there you find him
in his raw flayed skin
yearning for your embrace

arms around yourself
freed at last to love him.

xi

Remember what Father Lazarus quietly said
If I pray, then everyone prays
the secret he knows as far away
as he can get from the world, and the hundred monks
below him in St Anthony's Monastery.

High in his desert cave where he waits
the war within him lost and won
through all his silent days, until we're saved
with all the innocent humour of a real saint
he knows we are One.

xii

Staying in the truth
of what needs to be spoken
even as you fear to speak it

                              trusting

in one who knows

who feels
it is true
and so stands.

Our arms opening out as we dance
encircling the globe of your face
like a Moon Gate opening, an O
of new possibility

and later, in a lyrical chaos
your arms' rapid mirroring

                          this

image of a swan's feather, like a quill
and something as deep in the ground
you anchor to in your queenliness: and how

to tell you is
to Be Now

xiii

Move, be
the mountain moving
as you need to –

Dancing In Mountain
free for your life

easing your belly
of its bloated pain

throwing off the melancholy
of your regrets

to travel light, and lighter still
fast, fluid, free –

126

to disidentify
as deeply

rising into the newness

of another moment's smile.

xiv

… and even as your illusions die
it might be understanding
that staying on the mountain
means staying in life

as you climb
into your sun-thrown shadow

realizing all the things
you have not resolved

the knots that keep you
in life, still tied

(where someone even younger
might be released)

in the fusion of being and body
this interface, coal face
of the soul's own scripture

staying upright
in all
      that 'vertical'
           means

xv

for a dancer

Releasing light to the day
and all expectation

I can be patient, and I can hear
larks singing above your head in the blue

and you
can be at ease
lover of the rain, in full sun
and you can start to feel
as strangely, who you are with me

and we
can climb the gate back
having let go of time enough
to find ourselves walking arm in arm
at our single height

and we can be
breathed in by the third between us

that has all the space it needs
to play its silent, glad-filled song.

xvi

At all this height
among all these barren rocks and grass
one white flower
one star-white flower
as tiny as wood sorrel. Kindness.

And come the day
when we are far apart
will there be peace
between our hearts?

For shame of lack of kindness.

Oh desolate mountain
you know only this

what we bring
is all there is.

One tiny white flower
borne on the wind
and all the waste of what's between
that denied it.

xvii

for L.

Slow grief like dark honey dripping
calling you back to itself
mutely appearing …

But to hear you free
dancing in the wind and rain
as your message bleeps

frees me – in that instant
the weight released
lifting off my shoulders
beyond all blame
and expectation

beyond our story
in all its right and wrong
the end is freedom
and that we can be free

meaning *we are more*, and as alive
as when we first met
even though that moment's
gone for ever

there is this irreducible mystery

that as you free yourself, you free me
and we are each other's liberation.

xviii

And freedom can become love
but not if we refuse to forgive
its opening evaporates: and the whole sky
that's given closes on a locked egoic door.

Past or future; it doesn't matter
love's treasure is only found
when the heart opens beyond all reason

steadfast as its Red Mountain
where there is a sun that never goes down.

xix

Arunachala

Where did Ramana go
when he sat on the mountain?
Somewhere we cannot see
the other side of sunlight
surrendering himself entirely.

Forty years passing
staying on the mountain
bringing people there.

Where?

And it's the same calm
fearless question you ask
walking all round it
and up to the shrine

looking back towards it
in the amber dawn light.

What was your intent?
Was it only for a spiritual
pat on the head?

Ramana might smile and say
that's what you came for
not the pat on the head
but to ask this question

to no longer have to be
a safe believer
but instead to be yourself
inside all questions.

coda

for Eileen

Walking in the mountains here, you tell me
when you saw the mist clear
revealing its steep sheer rising
you saw the face of God unveiled ...
and as slowly hidden again.

You've fallen in love with mountains
great things that don't let you down.
'Be my rock!' you laugh out loud
changeless in the midst of change
and mirroring your own constancy, meaning

you can love again allowing the other to be
what we must all be in the end.

Holyhead, Llanfairfechan, and Stroud

7

Sinai

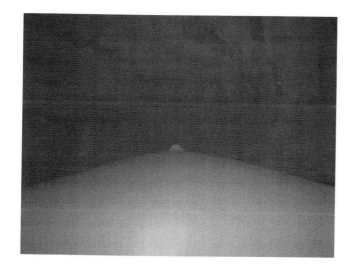

desert fast and desert feast

for Danny Shmulevitch, Satish Kumar,
the Class of 2010,
and Joanna Hicks

THE JOURNEY

At Sharm-el-Sheikh, surrounded by fake green
there are more lawn sprinklers than you've ever seen
just to reassure the tourists that this
isn't really a desert. It's an oasis!

Our Bedouin driver knows better
in this brief excursion into the unreal world.
He knows that what you see
is as important as what you say.

The resort from the air: tiny white apartments
flanked by turquoise paddling pools …
It looks like child's play

And the plastic detritus as if left by an invisible wave
crowds the central reservation in the dust
but our eyes are on mountains
rising in a cloud of light

scored in petrified earth like dried clay
in a landscape where nothing is hidden.

It all begins to fall away

Pylons, like frozen dalek dancers
breeze block shelters and lines of washing
the light slowly draining from the land
as the road empties with its vaguely familiar signs.

Bored Egyptian guards as the road forks to Dahab
past caring about the enemy

then the signal goes
as we begin to fall quiet

already shedding a layer
closer to silence.

The desert knows

There is another kind of life
beyond the road

… so that when we abruptly arrive
nowhere in the dark to find
an open-backed pick-up and a 4×4
waiting to transfer us and our luggage

we plunge into the unknown across the sand
without a clue where we're going – even
the ghost of previous tyre tracks are misleading
as we swerve to the left or right as suddenly

accelerating, lurched forward, to stop
the wheels getting snagged … then racing downhill
as crazily like a wild drive home
from a pub that doesn't exist

drunk on pure mysterious darkness

until we see ahead a solitary white figure
stand in the pale emerging moonlight
by a tethered camel … and we're finally out of time.

FIRST SILENCE

Finally we all stop talking.
Soft moonlight on sand
beneath our hands and feet
and the silence, a soft suspended hiss
spreading to everything you can see
shadowed in the moonlight
beyond the other sound you realize
is the blood pumping in your ears ...

and as you breathe into the softest hint of a breeze

this giant sleeping seal of rock
shouldering up beside us

everything here held in God's peace.

BEDOUIN TENT

Woven from the finest hessian
by the women in black bowed in burqas
only their eyes free in their slits –
recycled guy ropes and smoothed tree limbs for poles
set in a big rectangle with cloth mats for a floor
with their bright coloured strips, Moroccan-style
at the threshold where you remove your shoes

and inside, round a fire set in a circle of flat stones
sitting on thin mattresses, we're together
not raised apart on chairs, but cross-legged
at one in the unity of being human here
with nothing but our unpacked luggage
and only what our being can afford
by being in this pausing that is presence
where eyes come before words

and by the fire, candles in cut-off plastic bottles
half filled with sand (nothing is wasted)
and beside the blackened kettle full of karkaday
poured into small glass tumblers on a tray
and a single acacia log smouldering like a big cigar
spelling the scarcity of wood, conserved
like water, food, petrol, everything
held for what it is when you have nothing
but what you actually need.

Out of the darkness and the sand like a miracle
the cry of *soup!* delicious green smooth
and rice yellowed with saffron
from a kitchen that's like a ruin with no roof
a wall against the wind where our barefoot hosts
chop and stir unseen as the women

bearing the blackened pots over yards of sand
sitting to one side as we circle the fire
only later when we're gone surrounding its embers
with a meditation where cigarette follows cigarette
sucked in over the emptiness of the breath.

DESERT STARS

Not overlarge, flickering and dancing like tinsel lights
in your fantasy of what they would be like
you realize is mostly air pollution
but still bright, pellucid as you've never seen them
precise to the naked eye
as acupuncture points, incised
visible, mappable (as they were to us)
and filling the dark crystalline sky
in all the directions of your neck
craned and tilted as you lie back
between two rocks on a sleeping bag;

and if all their light reaching us now
left when we were together then
we're no less apart across all these miles, only held
with an intention we can't finally see
until it shines in our hearts and eyes
and all we're here to be.

SECOND SILENCE

Out of the noonday heat under a rocky overhang
we line up under to squat, in the relative cool
as the silence takes us again, its soft sibilance
become the sea sounding in your ears
the ancient sea that filled
all these wadis and gullies
before the hills and cliffs were scraped to stone …

and in the stillness now, the desert
stealing up like a snake hissing close
suffusing your chest as your eyes begin to close …

DESERT VAGINA

Open, wide open in the rock
poised above the dry hot noonday wadi
half hidden above eye level where you have to climb
where it wrinkles and cracks –

                             and there's her cave
open, breathtaking, unashamed

heart-shaped
                the size of a man
in the inner fluted folds of her flesh
sketched between sand-brown and red ochre
reaching back into the womb of the cliff
beyond all contradiction –

so all you can do is bow
wordlessly asking for rebirth as you enter
where heart and sex are one again …

                        and slowly turning
to re-emerge into the light
in the midst of all your self-conscious smiling
ask yourself: how do you want to be now?

HOW TO RIDE A CAMEL

Having straddled the saddle, and legs splayed
been hoisted up vertical –
as he or she (is it?) begins to move, and you get
tipped forward into your pelvis
tempted to grip on with your legs –
don't do it!

This is where riding is dancing instead.
Hang on to the pommel, yes
but for the rest
slip gently into your lower back
letting your spine be liquid
and move as she (he) moves

swaying to that rhythm
that is camel step, all day
across the open desert plain – then, hey!
you could even take the reins.

CATHEDRAL OF THE BREAST

1

First glimpsed in the moonlight
under the cliff's hollowed overhang
impossibly, improbably, this
sand-smooth wind-sculpted
– in a precise wind tunnel location –
the whispered sand grains spiralling
into a perfect full breast
topped by a nipple of rock
four foot by three

and in its cathedral
nave, altar and font.

2

You call it the Cathedral of the Breast
this one woman naked church
where you spent your fasting days
(and mostly naked).

It's a climb up the dune from camp
past a halfway clump of broom.

Breast in delicious early sun
(breast in all lights and seasons)
and the cavity behind it
a wall to lean against with its interior
so like peeling plaster
in this vast ancient niche

and above, at the hill mountain's peak
the eyes of an eagle, beak
worn smooth, filed by wind
but the eyes forever seeing.

3

A naked man closens
under his few remaining clothes.

He pauses at the threshold
then makes his way round, making sure
to leave her shape untrodden.

He leans against the hollowed rock
slowly surrendering all inward striving
into being held from behind
deeply as his spine can release
falling softly backwards into time
resting his neck on its effortless
exact pillar of stone.

He rests his whole being in creation
that is the createdness inside each cell of him
held by an eternal lover
he never knew he had
and never thought he knew.

A little later he leans forward
and spreads his arms lying
his cheek pillowed against her.

Now rest and feed from the breast;
rest and suck to your heart's content.

4

He could rest for hours, for days even
and can for as long as he needs to
but another voice is calling him
down to the rocks below
into the sun and the wide open wadi
where there's no visible form
and the wind blows.

It says *I am the Father
and you are my son. Will you come?*

IN THE SILENCE

1

We gather at the cliff's edge
wrapped in coats or blankets.
Cool dawn light. Pink clouds rising
over the wadi, over the ancient cracked hills.

This fasting now, entering silence
inside our bodies and all we can see
having only this.

And you are here invisibly
as only your soul can be
to spur me gently on.

And when I ask in Your Name
for the best we can be
finding each other again

a bird directly ahead
following the line of the cliff's edge
its wingbeats breaking the silence …

letting it be in freedom.

2

She's walking over the wadi below
all the way to her chosen place
like an altar under its table of rock –
sleeping bag draped over her shoulder
in side profile

at this distance, like some marvellous magical horse.

3

How to be with the time
what to do when there is nothing to do
and nowhere to go but here: when the hours
expand like inflated air with no limit
but the sun's orbit in a cloudless sky
inching its way around the horizon
your only punctuation, these signs of water
your only structure, this unfolding moment
your only company, your own acceptance
of loneliness transformed into intuiting a way.

4

Sweet Sinai silence, your soft hiss
as if of wind and sand, but invisible
and intangible, high in the inner ear;
surf braking on an unknown shore
closer to you than your own hand;
and as the morning sun warms your skin
penetrating every pore: the wind
still gently cool and soothing
the flies barely beginning
above the deep silence under it all.

5

There is only one answer to fear
and it's this: *anything could happen anyway*
regardless of your anxiety –
in spite of you, above you, and beyond you
(remember the way you both first magically met)
and only if you can surrender to *that*
will you ever have a moment's peace.

There is no other way, it means
you have to believe.

6

Two stories side by side:
the ego's bitter narration
based on cynical explanation
reduced to selfish motivation

and the Self's – initiation
threshold, invitation, expansion
when I invite you to Love
as you invite me to Freedom

and the tables at the feast
are trying to meet.

7

See how I am holding you now you say
in this beautiful morning sun
with a full breast of sand beside me
and the view down to the wadi below
still in exquisite etched brown shadow …

and all is well as it can only be now
there is nowhere else where you can be free
outside of this Yes in your body.

8

And it's yes to me – not someone else's idea
about how I should be in this precious time.
The camel's attenuated growling snort
waking me to where my No is
in the heart of freedom

and what it means to step outside
the ideology and the tribe
and be this I

crossing the wadi just in time
in the deepening gold evening light
to climb into an alcove in the cliff

for long enough to pray
as the sun silhouettes these jagged high worn faces
find me here as only I can be
stripped to myself in this human body
speaking the truth of its need.

9

Where the thin path among cliff-tumbled stones
under its towering overhang reaches its edge:
a flat boulder you crouch down on
to step into a gap between the rocks
lowering yourself down these handmade steps

into its wind-shielded opening
a shallow grave open to the sky
its curved weathered sandstone walls filled
with miniature alcoves and recesses
bordered by thin stalactites …

A sleeping bag on a thin mat stretches the length
before more rough steps down to the open edge
where my night-time visitor will rustle and climb
sensing food through layers of tin foil and plastic
while its occupant secretly sickens unto death
rushing out among the rocks to defecate
the cold wind wrapping round his legs.

10

A glimpse of a desert father
spelling out the name 'Aloysius'
a white patrician face in profile ...

'Submit to the will of the father': what does it mean?
To go into the direction of Self, he says
Self and strength. And from within your own freedom

when I can choose to surrender to be.

11

Allowing the Self to speak ... alive to its whispers
that bird's cliff-edge flight –
the sound of a bucket put down
you walking far down slowly in the light
picking your way over the cracked paving ...

the call of the desert clarified
to be naked to this

and then sitting, back against the ancient cliff
becoming the silence in the silent mind
expanding slowly becoming the sky

when a fluttering suddenly in front of my face
eyes filled with it, black against the light
streaked in gold ... for long enough to see

how it spells freedom to chrysalis me.

12

Stand in strength with the father
But I don't feel strong
Just give your attention to me
How?
By giving me your senses

And not giving them to a woman all the time
however beautiful she is, because
it means my awareness is leaving me

empty with longing.

Empty of you.

13

'Doing one thing at a time'
is how it's described in Zen
– as empowered action.
Sit up, drink water.
Prepare portable hand mirror.
Clean hands, lick fingers clean of sand.
Kneel. Undo lens case.
Peer into mirror, arse in the air.
Insert lens free of sand.
Blink. Try again.
Try the other eye.

Look around you.
How does it feel?
Suncream, clothing. Sunhat, head torch.
Toothbrush. Mouthwash. Water store. Loo roll.
The essentials are everywhere
dusted by silica
saying *be with me now.*

14

No strength at all
and it's there we descend
down sand slope in shelving rock
step by step to stand on the valley floor
suddenly unable to go on
(the sick bug biting, draining
every last ounce –) and feeling
for just a bit of shade out of the sun
to crawl in under this overhang
and die quietly ... letting go at last

and all of it to be brought this low
into the foundations of surrender
eye-level to sand: to stir, turn
and see these tiny white open flowers
blossoming out of nothing
but the vaguest memory of rain
                                        and to see
that's why I came.

15

Where water gushes forth
where's that? No rod, no rock
to strike ... and as hard to feel

held in all this dryness, so dry –
until you see the signs are small
and the desert's secret life
as discreet as it is vast ...
then you can know it all.

16

Death calls.

There among the sandstone stalactites
alcoves and holes in the shelving rock
as your eyes wander, can you see him?
Staring eye sockets and nose, domed forehead
and his mouth, well, grinning!

As unmistakeable as his meaning
Don't take all this too seriously
you know, I didn't either
and look where it got me ...

17

After the Dark Night comes the morning
after every inch of self-care
the blanket folded against the cliff
vaulting into the blue above, and You
all around me everywhere as light
and soft, not burning if I could
just breathe that in and let it be
the balm it is with nothing to do
but be the light ...

if only I could.

18

So You show me ... from far beyond my hands
and all my mind can reach
as I walk back unexpectedly to my cell ...

this single tiny something floating down
and flickering alive on the sandy floor, as I stoop
a miniature wingfeather

just like the one I sent you before leaving
returning as if at last, from you
(and in your own self and darker colour)

as if to say *I am with you* – beyond all my disbelief
'to help you on your way today'
having proved the existence of grace.

19

The wadi in light opening up like a cloudscape
into its furthest reaches between its craggy, cracked
hill mounds and mountains

after this little heart valley you show me
with its holding
its red and white fragments all over
the canvas of the ground ...
and the artefacts you'd made

for each other in the silence, as signs
this heart of pebbles enclosing sand
still intact, only its side wall breached
still breathing the desert air

to see what love can make, even in privation
and because of it – the heart breathing in
then expanding all over the golden evening sky

with its silent trumpet of release and joy.

20

Sensing you out there in the dark
for this last night under your lid of stone
I light this candle in its sawn-off bottle
and place it up on the parapet edge.

One light in all the wilderness dark
until, with a white flickering, your torch answers!
Across half a mile – and again
and I know you know that I know

and light to light, we're smiling
as the darkness becomes your face, friend
in my mind as I am in yours
as the full moon rises, calling us

to dream in the mystery again.

SANDBATH

No water, no mirror
but sand – imagine. Can you?
Washing yourself in sand?

Not wet sand or estuary mud
but the finest hourglass silica
running free in your hands.

Rub it on your skin and discover
it's perfect – smoothly abrasive, scaling
all your skin needs to shed

from neck to feet, beginning
so intimate a thing, then
to shed your clothes in the sun

and move from toes to ankle
to shin, calves and thigh
as the sand falls away unscathed

unpolluted by suds or discoloured water
evaporating its working in the sun
its tiny particles of shaving

even your chest hair, rubbed free
clings on to none of it
falling back near the sheltering cliff

and then pour this
delicious warm herbal mixture
as an after-rinse gleaming in the sun

as it oils down over you
a miracle out of a Schweppes bottle
celebrating your nakedness

shadow-flung in a single
unbroken line – your body
naked and free, all one, complete

with the rock and the sand, and
just then ... as you stand to dry
a butterfly comes

your salutation: drifting, flitting
among these tiny white flowers
free as necessity, free as the day.

DESERT STONES

Creamy white quartz, smoothed to a sheen. Precious wadi
pearls.

White sandstone balls, constantly rolled like dough dusted
in silica: in all sizes from plump cherry to tennis ball.

Red mauve terracotta and gold ochre sand-hand painted
cave token.

A heart of gold, out of the blue, glancing down: deep cut
sandstone with an imperial yellow topping.

A jawbone of ironstone, a blunt forgotten instrument
(so many other skulls long since turned to dust).

Quartz superglued by heat to sandstone, a tiny summit of
illumination.

A triangle of white silica topped with menstrual red ochre.

A snapped off meteorite fragment with its cold creased
metallic skin, and white crystal flesh like coconut.

A granite chip that is salmon pink and silica white
everywhere containing the seeds of its own dissolution.

A fragment of what could have been pottery but never
was.

A heat-basted silica heart like an oyster.

A stone of sand, variegated with light and dark bands, and
so sunbaked it crumbles to the touch like a biscuit.

Top of the mountain: a flat piece of limestone from the ancient seabed at nine hundred metres that is a house with one window.

Broken from the underlayer, the wadi within the wadi, the hidden foundations: pale mauve streaked under white with a single gold painted line, and so light to hold it only weighs of air.

WILDERNESS WALK

After all this silence
we fill the wilderness with our stories
we fill the sun-baked emptiness as we walk now
leaving the camp behind;
the tent stripped of its mats gone on ahead
as we wander in home valley vastness
our precious lives etched in their colours
hovering hummingbird-bright
as the beach-like sand absorbs our steps

And behind us, briefly cruising, a jeep
white-dwarfed under the ancient cliffs
disgorges its transient visitors
for their tiny instant of time
before it revs on soundlessly by ...

and we move on under their cracked expanse
suspended in their time of sand
slow as erosion, built for millennia
into the farthest reaches of our spirit
that can conceive of being here this long
being alive this long, in any dimension
stretching our imagining to breaking ...

for as long as they wandered, and we do
across the open plain where distance retreats
and the mountain you're reaching towards
remains the same, as in a dream of walking
where you move like a mime artist on the spot
and the cliffs that tower above us are as impassive
with their massive featureless heads
where nothing matters to the eagle but the view

and I pray for us, so fragile down below
with this chalk scratched triangle
encasing its round white stone
that we may find the love that's holding us
again so we can let go –

As we step onto the Broken Plain
where the orange-red scree fragments spread
the hills ahead as if quarry-blasted with explosions
mirrored by the mottled cloud-sky

and the kneeling waiting camels gift our feet
raised into their swinging siesta step;
and Marbruk, who knows this way so well
tolerates his temporary janitor whose name
keeps slipping away like sand grains;
but the barefoot Bedouin boy by his side
shall pass through the eye of the needle
because he leads his camel kindly

As you guide us on foot into Asteroid Valley
where these frozen star-flung fragments landed
their wrinkled metallic skin still cool to the touch
their white crystal inner flesh like coconut
as other as only the universe can be
all around this tiny vast domain
where wilderness planets weave without end
and we carry its testimony

out to where this peeled rock phallus rises to the sky
without apology, just being as we are
in our primordial nature as the blood
floods us as created man and woman
surviving all these hundreds of thousands of years
by nothing less definite

and on the plain, just the sketch of a path
a thin ribbon in the emptiness
as we walk with our stories and our silence
and for a moment in the midst of your telling
glancing up at you ahead, in your walking
on in the swaying of your camel
just floating timeless in your motion
a mirage imprinted on the air
where you can't tell what day or year it is –

The desert hills ahead folded into the blue
their late sun streaming over the sand
almost white in the light
among the footprints and the camel prints side by side;

and the sun as it will be setting, poised
a huge translucent amber balloon of light
between the ridges and the dunes;

and the moon rising, vertically as bright
full as my whispered aching for you
where the tyre tracks lead out into the midnight …

the pitted rocks full of their own secrets
the camels resting in their silhouettes
eight bodies breathing in line in the nomad tent.

BARAKA

A dune reaches nearly halfway from the plain
massed against the mountainside
breaking into clear dry boulders for hands and feet.
And climbing means now in the given time
to shed your lunar melancholy, perhaps
and the sickness and doubt of the days
to reach for the sun.

Dawn our calling with no breakfast
the pure opposite of rest
lungfuls of air for the dune
on this ascent to the old seabed.

And the climbing is easy, no vertical walls
or dizzying drops, just the present moment
of touching the mountain's body
holding us as nearly as it can
in the dry warm stillness as we wind round.
And if this was Your Body? I'd say it is.

The summit up ahead above scree
in its once submerged limestone high and dry
as an ark ... for us to lie down on dreaming
where our breath meets the sky
recalling our aquatic origin.

How many millennia has it been?
And our bodies still remember
the way our bones sing to the desert silence.

We lie around gladly stranded
before standing as we are now
to face Saudi Arabia
Sinai veiled in a blue mist
Cairo across that parallel ridge

Jerusalem beyond the sun
where the Promised Land was a dream
of Your Kingdom within.

Eden within, earth heart
where our hearts return
from all our mind's wandering.
Forty years or centuries.

And now in this moment of loving
to want you here –
arrowbright across the miles
to where you might be waking
as we did on our new day's morning.

Dawn our eyes, our traveller's eyes
seeing us as always for the first time
and the last time in this moment
expanding in all directions
with more than can ever be held
holding us in its life
become a traveller's tale.

And here and now beyond all distance
(where the desert is beyond distance)
I stand in the consciousness that can stretch
forever surpassing itself, like this view;
which is why we climb mountains
to come down with a more generous truth.

ADUDA DUNE

Trudging up to where the line
is as crisp as on a folded sheet, rippled
in its wave-scales of sand-sea moving
heaped into this

three hundred foot tsunami
poised above the granite it has
as unbelievably come from
as hard as it is soft –
dark as this is light –
craggy black spread ranging below

And all you can do
is stand in wonder, waiting to let go
down its ski-less slope
walking, running, rolling as you wish
as you untie your boots
on this last threshold
of all your being
offered to lightness and air
freedom and laughter
to be reborn like this
like a second chance.

You wait for your moment.
You step out

and as one foot lifts and softly ignites after the other

in a sole-kissed sliding slalom all the way down

you dance.

coda

Everything returns to desert sleep
the Bedouin to a secret place to die
the camel, after years of service, released
left to wander at will; and as you close your eyes
in afternoon weariness and lie down
where the sand takes you as the hills do
in their skeletal embrace, *I know you*
they say without words or need of them
in the silence that knows what it is;
and beneath our departing plane now
as you keen your eyes through its window-slit
the desert a dream under the dusky gold light
folded back into the contours of its mysteries
wadi after nameles wadi, hill, mountain
beyond wherever you thought you were
where you also have left no trace behind.

Afterword

IN FLOW

for Angela

You are in bed as I call. And here
the water is pouring in the darkness from the lips
of this flow-form as each petalled layer
swings its content back and forth
two sides of a vesica, making love, infinite.
I hold the phone to the water, you all ear.

The great sycamore rises lit as if in moonlight
from the house's adjacent porch light
like the Tree of Life itself; trunk and branches soaring,
    strong.
I wander down the dark incline of the grass
as we talk of the heart, its tentative reaching
as clear in what it knows; your face there
luminous and bright, known and unknown.

The light in your voice, your words
as lucid because they're you, I tell you
as we pause before we say goodnight … and still
the water is sounding as you settle
stretching your body invisibly and turning
into the woman-waters of your sleep.

Hawkwood

165

the journey continues …

Acknowledgements and Notes

My thanks especially to Kevan Manwaring and Anthony Nanson with this bardic Awen imprint I'm so glad to be a part of, with its ecocentric vision at the green heart of where we are. All the work selected here from over twenty years is chosen with the Awen vision in mind, from my own love of wild places – places of truth.

Trwyn Meditations was first published by Charles Thomson at Victoria Press in 1987. Some extracts subsequently appeared in *Kingdom of the Edge: selected poems 1980–1998* (Element, 1999). Plas Penrhyn near Penrhyndeudraeth, North Wales, was the home of both Elizabeth Gaskell and, later, Bertrand Russell. The isolated cottage that is Trwyn Penrhyn is down through the woods beyond Portmeirion, opposite Porthmadog and facing Borth-y-Gest across the Traeth Mawr (Great Sands).

Section 6 of 'By the Shores of Loch Awe' appeared in *With My Heart in My Mouth* (ed. Paul Matthews, Rudolf Steiner Press, 1994) and *Kingdom of the Edge.* My thanks to John Mingay, who displayed the complete poem on his Raunchland Publications website in 2003, where it's still to be found in the archive selection, along with 'Ardnamurchan in Blue' from 1997.

'The Oak' refers to the sixth-oldest oak in England, to be found on the Blow Estate behind Edge Farm, near Painswick, Gloucestershire.

'The Sacred Way' was commissioned by Martin Palmer/ICOREC for his book *Sacred Britain: a guide to the sacred sites and pilgrim routes* (Piatkus, 1997), where it runs in sections under the eighteen chapter heads. The last part has also been published in *The Heart's Ragged Evangelist: love poems for the greater love* (PS Avalon, 2005).

'The Invitation' was written while I was poet-in-residence at St James's Church, Piccadilly (2005–6). The contrast between Culbone in its deep hidden valley and Piccadilly in central London could not be more meaningfully extreme.

My thanks to Jenny Davis for first taking me to Culbone in 1989 while we were collaboratng on *Journey to Eden* (Eden Centre Books, 1991).

'According to the Place' draws on Joan Cooper's *Culbone: a spiritual history* (Georjan Studio, 1977) as its primary source. Some of her books and pamphlets are still in print (enquiries to Jeff and Jen Cox, Culbone Trust, 01643 862959 or Barrie O'Connor – see below). Joan Cooper's *The Door Within* and *Corner Stones of the Spiritual World* are also both recommended reading.

Certain specific dates are alluded to in 'According to the Place'. Christ's visit to Culbone (xi) as part of his legendary visit to the west of Britain with his uncle Joseph of Arimathea was in A.D. 25. Columba's landing on Iona (xiv) was in 563. The last leper in England (xx) died in 1621. Shelley's death (xxiii) was in 1822. The famous and the unknown are deliberately juxtaposed in my text, asserting our common (and mortal) humanity.

If you wish to stay for longer than a day at Culbone, on retreat in simple accommodation, you can apply in writing to Barrie O'Connor, The Lodge, Culbone, Porlock Weir, Somerset, TA24 8PQ, stating your reason and giving your contact details. You can, alternatively, stay just above the valley at either Ash Farm or Silcombe Farm (B&B).

In 'The Mountain', 'call of the mountain' (iii) refers to Benazir Bhutto's assassination in Pakistan (28 December 2007). The first of the 'two mountains' is outside Holyhead, Anglesey; the second in the Aber Valley near Llanfairfechan. In 'staying on the mountain', (v) refers to writer, poet, and Zen practitioner Henry Shukman; (vi) to poet/artist Marion Fawlk; (viii) to a remark made to me by Richard Wainwright (Jungian analyst); (xi) to the memorable *Extreme Pilgrim* Channel 4 series with Peter Owen Jones (February 2008); and (xix) to Ramana Maharshi – and Timothy Glazier, who visited his sacred mountain and told me his story.

In Sinai, thanks to Danny Shmulevitch, I was a guest of the Makhad Trust, which supports the Bedouin people in reclaiming and conserving their habitat. On Satish Kumar's 'Desert Fast, Desert Feast' retreat in March 2010 (which included a three-day water fast), my commission was to write a series of poems and also to take photographs for the website to encourage more people to visit and experience this unique environment. We were right out in the desert; we also followed the Exodus route, and Danny was our unfailing guide, first encountered in the moonlight at the end of the first poem in the sequence.

Also available from Awen Publications:

Tidal Shift: selected poems
Mary Palmer

Knowing her end was near, Mary Palmer worked on her poems, compiling her very best and writing new ones with a feverish intensity. This is the result, published here with her cooperation and consent. These are poems from the extreme edge and very centre of life – words of light that defy death's shadow with a startling intensity, clarity, and honesty. Containing poems from across Mary's career, selected by Jay Ramsay, *Tidal Shift* is an impressive legacy from a poet of soul and insight.

'She has the courage to confront struggles and sickness, the world's and her own. Unpious but radically spiritual, she stays faithfully questioning right to the end.' *Philip Gross*

Poetry ISBN 978-1-906900-09-0 £9.99

The Fifth Quarter
Richard Selby

The Fifth Quarter is Romney Marsh, as defined by the Revd Richard Harris Barham in *The Ingoldsby Legends*: 'The World, according to the best geographers, is divided into Europe, Asia, Africa, America and Romney Marsh.' It is a place apart, almost another world. This collection of stories and poems explores its ancient and modern landscapes, wonders at its past, and reflects upon its present. Richard Selby has known Romney Marsh all his life. His writing reflects the uniqueness of The Marsh through prose, poetry, and written versions of stories he performs as a storyteller.

Fiction/Poetry ISBN 978-0-9546137-9-2 £9.99
Spirit of Place Volume 2

Soul of the Earth: the Awen anthology of eco-spiritual poetry
edited by Jay Ramsay

Beautifully crafted, yet challenging received wisdom and pushing boundaries, these are cutting-edge poems from a new generation of writers who share a love of the Earth and haven't given up on humans either. In poems as light as a butterfly and as wild as a storm you'll find vivid, contemporary voices that dare to explore a spiritual dimension to life on Earth and, in doing so, imply that a way out of our global crisis of ecological catastrophe, financial meltdown, and bankruptcy of the spirit is to look beyond the impasse of materialism. With contributions from poets in the USA, Canada, UK, Australia, and New Zealand, this anthology reaches out across the planet to embrace the challenges and blessings of being alive on the Earth in the twenty-first century.

'All real poetry seeks to "renew the face of the earth" – and so to resist the exploiting, banalization or defacing of what lies around us. I hope this collection will serve the renewal of vision we so badly need.'
Most Revd Dr Rowan Williams

Poetry ISBN 978-1-906900-17-5 £11.99

The Immanent Moment
Kevan Manwaring

The sound of snow falling on a Somerset hillside, the evanescence of a waterspout on a remote Scottish island, the invisible view from a Welsh mountain, the light on the Grand Canal in Venice, the fire in a Bedouin camel-herder's eyes … These poems consider the little epiphanies of life and capture such fleeting pulses of consciousness in sinuous, euphonic language. A meditation on time, mortality, transience, and place, this collection celebrates the beauty of both the natural and the man-made, the familiar and the exotic, and the interstices and intimacy of love.

Poetry ISBN 978-1-906900-41-0 £8.99

Iona
Mary Palmer

What do you do when you are torn apart by your 'selves'? The pilgrim poet, rebel Mordec and tweedy Aelia set sail for Iona – a thin place, an island on the edge. It's a journey between worlds, back to the roots of their culture. On the Height of Storm they relive a Viking massacre, at Port of the Coracle encounter vipers. They meet Morrighan, a bloodthirsty goddess, and Abbot Dominic with his concubine nuns. There are omens, chants, curses … During her stay Mordec learns that words can heal or destroy, and the poet writes her way out of darkness. A powerful story, celebrating a journey to wholeness, from an accomplished poet.

'Always truthful, this poetry confronts both beauty and ugliness and makes space for light to slip between the two.' *Rose Flint*

Poetry ISBN 978-0-9546137-8-5 £6.99 Spirit of Place Volume 1

Crackle of Almonds: selected poems
Gabriel Bradford Millar

In these renegade poems ranging from 1958 to 2011 Gabriel Bradford Millar presents a spectrum of life, in all its piquant poignancy, with unfaltering precision, defiance, and finesse. From the very first to the very last, the breathtaking skill of this consummate wordsmith does not waver. Many of the poems linger in the air – not least because Millar performs them orally with such verve. She believes 'that poems, like love-talk, should go from mouth to ear without any paper in between'. On the page their orality and aurality fragrance their presence without diminishing their literary elegance. Continually astonishing, these epicurean poems not only offer a lasting testimony to a 'life well-lived', but inspire the reader to live well too

'She does not just write *about* the world; she dips her syllables in the bitter sweet of its "gazpacho". She thinks melodically.' *Paul Matthews*

Poetry ISBN 978-1-906900-29-8 £9.99

An Ecobardic Manifesto: a vision for the arts in a time of environmental crisis
Fire Springs

What is the raison d'être of the arts in an age of global ecological crisis? In this audacious document, Fire Springs present a new vision for the arts, one that holds together commitment to artistic integrity and craftsmanship with responsiveness to the peculiar challenges of our time. Foremost among those challenges are the strained relationship between human beings and the ecosystem we inhabit and the vital need to sustain empathy for that which is other than ourselves. Fundamental to the arts' task in such an age is a willingness to embrace contradiction, not least the deepening polarisation between scientific and economic materialism and metaphysical sources of meaning and hope. This pamphlet is a clarion call to everyone working in the arts today who wants their efforts to make a difference.

Art Theory/Literary Criticism ISBN 978-1-906900-07-6 £2.50

The Firekeeper's Daughter
Karola Renard

From the vastness of Stone Age Siberia to a minefield in today's Angola, from the black beaches of Iceland to the African savannah and a Jewish-German cemetery, Karola Renard tells thirteen mythic stories of initiation featuring twenty-first-century kelpies, sirens, and holy fools, a river of tears and a girl who dances on fire, a maiden shaman of ice, a witch in a secret garden, Queen Guinevere's magic mirror, and a woman who swallows the moon. The red thread running through them all is a deep faith in life and the need to find truth and meaning even in the greatest of ordeals.

'In her lively and vivid stories, Karola Renard points a finger towards the mythic threads that run through life's initiations.' *Martin Shaw*

Fiction ISBN 978-1-906900-18-2 £9.99

Glossing the Spoils
Charlotte Hussey

In a glosa, an early Renaissance poetic form, tribute is paid to another poet. Each of these 28 modern glosa works like an intricate time-travel machine, carrying the reader back to the beginnings of Western European literature. Like a glass fairy bridge, its abutments decorated with goblins, trolls, incubi, and ever spiteful dragons, these poems vault over the violent currents of some fifteen hundred years. Anchored at one end in the deep past and at the other in the present, they explore interconnections between historical, personal, psychological, and mythic states. Plundering their opening passages from such ancient texts as *Beowulf*, *The Mabinogion*, and *The Tain*, these glosa give voice to the surreal potency of the Western European imagination.

Poetry ISBN 978-1-906900-28-1 £7.99

Dancing with Dark Goddesses: movements in poetry
Irina Kuzminsky

The dance is life – life is the dance – in all its manifestations, in all its sorrow and joy, cruelty and beauty. And the faces of the Dark Goddesses are many – some are dark with veiling and unknowing, some are dark with sorrow, some are dark with mystery and a light so great that it paradoxically shades them from sight. The poems in this collection are an encounter with many of these faces, in words marked with feminine energy and a belief in the transformative power of the poetic word. Spiritual and sexual, earthy and refined, a woman's voice speaks to women and to the feminine in women and men – of an openness to life, a surrender to the workings of love, and a trust in the Dark Goddesses and their ways of leading us through the dance.

'Potent, seminal, visionary.' *Kevin George Brown*

Poetry/Dance ISBN 978-1906900120 £9.99

Printed in Great Britain
by Amazon